Making Sense
of Scripture

Making Sense
of Scripture

Big Questions about the Book of Faith

David J. Lose

AUGSBURG FORTRESS
Minneapolis

MAKING SENSE OF SCRIPTURE
Big Questions about the Book of Faith

Book of Faith Adult Bible Studies

This book is accompanied by a Leader Guide and DVD. These resources are also available for purchase online at www.augsburgfortress.org.

Book of faith is an initiative of the
Evangelical Lutheran Church in America
God's work. Our hands.

For more information about the Book of Faith Initiative, go to www.bookoffaith.org

ISBN: 978-0-8066-9953-0

Editor: Scott Tunseth
Cover design: Spunk Design Machine, spkdm.com
Interior design: Ivy Palmer Skrade
Illustrations: Joe Vaughn

This book was typeset using Minion, Omnes and Paperback.

Library of Congress Cataloging-in-Publication Data
Lose, David J.
  Making sense of Scripture : big questions about the book of faith / David J. Lose.
     p. cm. -- (Book of faith adult Bible studies)
  Book is accompanied by a Leader guide and DVD.
  ISBN 978-0-8066-9953-0 (alk. paper)
  1. Bible--Miscellanea. I. Title.

BS612.L67 2009
220.6--dc22
                              2009012088

The paper used in this publication meets the minimum requirements of American National Standard for Information Sciences—Permanence of Paper for Printed Library Materials, ANSI Z329.48–1984.

Manufactured in the U.S.A.

15   14   13   6   7   8   9   10   11   12

Contents

Acknowledgements vii

Introduction 1

Chapter **1**: What Is the Bible? 11

Chapter **2**: Is the Bible True? 33

Chapter **3**: How Is the Bible the Word of God? 55

Chapter **4**: Where Did the Bible Come From? 81

Chapter **5**: How Can I Read the Bible with
Greater Understanding? 111

Chapter **6**: Is There a "Center" to Scripture? 143

Chapter **7**: What Kind of Authority Does the Bible Hold? . . 179

Conclusion 203

For Further Reading 205

Dedication

For John and Susan Lose, my parents,
who first placed a Bible in my hands and encouraged me to read . . .
. . . and to think!

Acknowledgements

There is a quotation by James Thurber that sums up my outlook on the life of faith as well as any other: "It is better to know some of the questions than all of the answers." Asking questions is the act of a restless and lively faith. But having—or at least believing one has—all the answers is not only static but infinitely boring. I have been blessed the past nine years to ask and discuss the great and small questions of faith and life with wonderful students and colleagues at Luther Seminary in St. Paul, Minnesota. Those conversations have greatly shaped many of the ideas that find expression in this book, and I am grateful to so many for their encouragement and camaraderie.

Three colleagues in particular have contributed their time, wisdom, and insight to improving this project. Karoline Lewis and Rolf Jacobson offered able help at several critical junctures, and Matt Skinner took time from his sabbatical to read and comment on the whole manuscript. These three are not only great friends but some of the best teachers and keenest minds in the church. If you ever have a chance to hear any of them speak or to read something one of them has written, do it! You will not be sorry.

The editors and staff at Augsburg Fortress have been supportive and wise. I would not have seen this project to fruition were it not for the encouragement of Tim Paulson and Kristofer Skrade and the judicious and patient editing and creativity of Scott Tunseth.

Because of the timeline for this project, my wife Karin and children Katie and Jack cheerfully endured longer absences from me than I hope to require again for quite some time. There is little, if anything, of value I could accomplish were it not for their love and support, and I thank God for them every day.

Above all I want to thank my parents, John and Susan Lose. Not only did they consistently encourage my questions, but they always seemed to know which ones to answer and which to leave for me to strive after. Their love and example has served me well beyond measure, and this book is dedicated to them with gratitude to God for their faithfulness.

Introduction

Do you remember the first time you picked up a book and couldn't put it down? For me it was C. S. Lewis's *The Lion, the Witch, and the Wardrobe*. For my kids it's been *Harry Potter and the Sorcerer's Stone*. For some, like me and my children, this happened in childhood. For others, it wasn't until much later in school, or even adulthood, when they picked up a book that captivated them for hours on end and launched their careers as readers.

What about you? Can you recall the first time you were so drawn into a story that everything around you seemed to recede into the background, and the characters of the book in your hands—and their challenges, opportunities, and dangers—became, at least for a little while, the most important thing to you?

With some books, of course, it's for more than a little while. Some books don't simply absorb you; they change you, altering the way you think and feel about some particular issue or even about life in general. Have you read a book like that? What was its name? How old were you when you read it? What about it so moved you that you remember it all these months or years later? Books, really good books, are powerful.

In the years leading up to the Civil War, *Uncle Tom's Cabin* was that kind of book. Harriet Beecher Stowe's 19th-century bestseller vividly depicted the cruelty of slavery and changed the way many Americans thought about African Americans and slavery. When Abraham Lincoln met Beecher he remarked, "So here's the little lady that started such a big war!" While not all great books have such dramatic consequences, really good books leave a mark upon their readers, changing them—and sometimes their generation—forever.

My guess is that you've had encounters with these kinds of books. That you've been not just touched but moved, drawn into the pages of a book so fully that you left your encounter changed. Maybe that's one reason why you're holding this book in your hands—you're a reader; you love books and know their power.

I'd also guess, though, that the Bible has *not* been one of those books for you. Go ahead, be honest. I know it's a little embarrassing to admit. After all, the Bible is supposed to be *the* Book. And, truth be told, it has been an incredibly popular and powerful book for centuries. (In fact, the only book that outsold *Uncle Tom's Cabin* in the 19th century was the Bible, and even today more copies are sold each year than any other book, even *Harry Potter*!) More importantly, though, many people testify how their lives have been transformed by reading the Bible.

Reading the "good book"

Still, not many of us would describe the Bible as a book "I just couldn't put down." I don't know how often I've asked students of all ages—in classes I've taught at seminary, churches, and summer camps—how many have tried to read the Bible through from beginning to end. Each time, a large number of hands go up in the air. When I ask how many actually have completed this project, however, very few hands remain. So let's face it: the Bible is challenging, even difficult reading, with strange names and customs on almost every page. It's filled with all kinds of literature we don't often encounter anywhere else. Within the pages of the Bible you'll find everything ranging from poetry to genealogies and parables to legal codes. Perhaps for this reason, many of us have had as many frustrating experiences with reading the Bible as we've had fruitful ones.

So most of us find ourselves in a dilemma about the "good book."

We know we should read the Bible, and maybe even have tried, but somehow we don't find ourselves pulled into its pages the way we have been by other books.

We want to read and enjoy the Bible, and are attracted to the promise that it might change our lives for the better, but haven't found this to be the case. Which is maybe another part of the reason you're considering reading this book—you, like countless other persons of varying degrees of faith or church experience, want very much to get a whole lot more out of reading the Bible than you have so far.

If this is the case, I've got good news for you: the Bible *is* an amazing book, difficult and complicated to be sure, but still amazing. There's a reason people have been reading and rereading it for thousands of years, and I've written this book to help you make sense of Scripture and join their number.

Making Sense of Scripture, I should be clear, is not a book *on* the Bible, in the sense that it attempts to give you the major plot line of the Bible or to cover all the individual books or parts within it. (There are very good books of that nature, and I've listed several at the end of the book.) Rather, it is a book *about* the Bible, explaining enough of the Bible's history and nature to make it more accessible to you. Even more, *Making Sense of Scripture* is a book on *how to read the Bible* in the first place, and I hope and intend that it will give you confidence to explore the actual content and claims of the Bible on your own or in study with others.

Toward that end, I use the conversations in the book to:

1. Present information about the Bible and the world it came out of;
2. Explain some of its more confusing elements; and
3. Set the Bible in its proper historical and literary contexts.

By doing these things, I hope to make reading the Bible a far more satisfying experience for you.

Of course, information about the Bible and its world and writers is only one part of the key to getting more from your reading. The other part is to make some sense of all the claims people make about the Bible. For whatever else the Bible does, it certainly arouses people's passions. Some claim it is the Word of God and that it is literally, factually true in every respect. Some believe it is true, but that it does not offer—and maybe never intended to offer—a historically or scientifically accurate account of the world. Still others believe the Bible is great literature and should be treated as such—that is, read as the sacred scriptures of one of the world's great religions, but as nothing more. To help you read the Bible successfully, I also use the conversations in the book to develop a theological framework that will enable you to:

1. Understand and take stock of the varied claims about the Bible; and
2. Come to your own judgments about what the Bible is and what you can expect from reading it.

Point of view

Here, though, I must be completely candid: there is no unbiased or completely objective reading of the Bible.

There is no unbiased or completely objective reading of the Bible.

Everyone reads from a point of view. I'll have more to say about that later, but for now, whether we like it or not, we need to admit that we won't ever be able to prove all the claims we make about the Bible. This is as true for the person who claims the Bible is God's "inerrant" Word as it is for the person who doesn't. Think about it. How would one prove—or disprove—such a claim in the first place? We may certainly have all kinds of good reasons for our beliefs. Even so, what we believe about the Bible and how it might affect us remains a matter of faith and conviction, not dispassionate fact. And this is as true for me as it is for you.

For this reason, throughout the book I will try to present different opinions about the Bible with some measure of objectivity, but it is important to remember that, at the end of the day, I will more often than not end up favoring one opinion over another. And while I will try to show you my rationale for the judgments I make, where I end up is as much a matter of conviction, belief, and faith as it is reason or intellect.

So keep that in mind: you are not getting an unbiased opinion on the matter (as if there is one out there!), but rather are receiving a point of view offered in the hope that it will shape and sharpen your own point of view so that you will read the Bible with more confidence and pleasure. Through this book, I hope to help you come to a better understanding of your own beliefs about the Bible by being in conversation with the beliefs and convictions, as well as the knowledge and insights, of the faith tradition I represent.

Bring your questions!

In the spirit of openness just mentioned, I should confess one of the major convictions behind this book. It's a conviction that not only influences both the content and shape of the book, but may also help you decide whether you want to keep reading. *I believe asking questions is essential to the life of faith.* Questions are not the mark of an inadequate faith but instead the mark of the kind of curious, searching, seeking faith that you find all over the pages of Scripture. If you are looking for all the answers, or hoping to find a view of Scripture as God's divine answer book, then this probably isn't the book for you. But if you believe, with me, that the Christian life should take seriously both our heads and our hearts, our doubts and our faith, and involves as many questions as it does answers, then I invite you to read on.

Because of the importance I place on questions, you'll notice immediately that the book revolves around them. Each chapter is structured around what I think are central questions about the Bible. The ongoing conversations within each chapter are fueled by many more questions. I rely on questions to advance the goal of this book for two reasons:

- Questions are, I think, the engine of all great conversations. The give and take of asking and trying to answer questions that matter to us helps us make sense of the world, and so why not also the Bible?
- Questions have the gift of nurturing curiosity in a way that flat statements and simple claims do not.

Rather than start with conclusions, I am inviting you to come along with me to engage the major questions about the Bible that people of good conscience and abundant curiosity often ask.

These questions don't come out of the blue. Not only have I regularly had my own share of questions about the Bible, but for quite some time when I've been out and about teaching on these things, I've asked folks about their experience of reading the Bible and invited them to name their deepest questions. What you see before you is the result of those years of dialogue. Some of the questions are combinations of related questions and concerns. Others are almost verbatim questions that were posed to me by a perceptive conversation partner.

I hope these questions get at some of your questions, and if you have others not touched upon here, please let me know. I've arranged these questions in an order that makes narrative sense to me and that I hope will guide you through some of the major facets of the Bible in a reasonably organized way. But if you see a question further down the book that grabs your attention more than the one I've put first, by all means feel free to jump ahead.

No experience needed

You may be wondering if you need to be familiar with the Bible to get something out of reading this book. The simple answer is no. But even if you are very familiar with it, I think you will discover lots of new questions and insights. Maybe you've heard the Bible read in church, or maybe you've read it in a high school literature class. Maybe you've studied the Bible for years, or maybe you haven't picked one up in decades. Maybe you know the Bible better than any other book you own, or maybe you heard the stories long ago but don't remember them very well. And—who knows?—maybe you're just wondering why people continue to make a big fuss over such an old book and want in on the action. No matter where you are, no matter how much or how little experience you have, I think you will find in this book engaging questions addressed in an honest and accessible way.

Ideally, we'd take up the questions in this book together in your living room or around my kitchen table. But since that isn't possible, I've tried to imagine how a conversation like this might go, and I've written the book in this way. You'll notice several things about this decision almost immediately. First, the tone throughout the book is pretty conversational, even informal. The examples I use are from everyday life, and the parts of Scripture I reference are pretty common.

Second, because I wanted this book to be a conversation, there are no footnotes. It's not that I don't like footnotes—we can learn a lot from other writers on these subjects, and I certainly have—but I think that in this case it will help just to talk these things through rather than reference other works. After reading this book, you may indeed be eager for more study, and I will provide a list of further resources at the end to help you get going. But for now, it's just us hashing these matters out together.

Third, there is room at the end of each chapter for you to jot down your own insights and questions. Feel free to write down the various things about the Bible and faith that occur to you, as well as note the ongoing or new questions you have. For that matter, feel free to mark up the book as much as you like. By taking note of what we're learning and still wondering about, we learn even more. This is your book now, so go to town.

High hopes and a warning

I have high hopes for this book. Or, to put it more clearly, I have two particularly high hopes for what you will get out of this book:

> *First, I hope that after reading this book you will understand enough about the Bible to help you penetrate through the years and cultures that separate us from it. I hope you will be absorbed by the Bible's stories in a way that will touch and move you, and maybe even transform the way you look at yourself, the world, and God.*

> *Second, I hope that you will discover that you can bring both your mind and your heart to the enterprise of reading the Bible. I hope you will feel free to think, wonder, question, and even express doubt as we discuss issues and explore the claims the Bible makes. And I hope and pray that through all the thinking, wondering, questioning, and doubting, you might also find the capacity to hear God speaking a word to you.*

As you can probably tell, I believe the Bible is a powerful book. More than that, I believe that through the Bible, God continues to speak to women and men today, and by speaking to them not only helps them make sense of their lives but also contribute to the well-being of their neighbor and the world.

I also believe that the God of Scripture invites us to engage the Bible with both our intellect and faith.

The God of Scripture invites us to engage the Bible with both our intellect and faith.

Too many views of the Bible seem to invite us to check our brains at the door, while others demand the same of our faith. But I don't think it has to be that way, and I've written this book to offer an alternative to the choices currently available.

One last thing before we get started. . . . I should offer you a warning, not unlike those offered by the Surgeon General: reading the Bible can be hazardous, not only to your health, but also to your wealth, reputation, and even your very life. Seriously. Over the centuries people who have read the Bible have been led to do things beyond their imaginations. Examples are too numerous and wide-ranging to name in detail, but a few possibilities come immediately to mind:

- making peace with someone who had formerly been an enemy;
- giving away one's wealth or security for the sake of another;
- leaving the comforts of home to reach out to others;
- changing careers to respond more fully to a sense of God's call;
- staying in one's career to do the same; or
- putting one's reputation, and even life, on the line by taking a stand for justice.

Sometimes these actions are quite dramatic. Other times they are fairly common, even everyday, but in each case they represent the actions of someone who has been marked, even changed, by reading the book of faith.

Before you begin

Okay, you've been warned. So now it's time to get going. But first, I want to suggest something. Before we start the conversation, take just a moment or two to think about your own thoughts and feelings about the Bible. Remember all the different claims I mentioned that people make about the Bible? Well, where do you find yourself in the mix? What kind of book do you think the Bible is? Is it sacred or secular, inspired or interesting? Does it reveal God's will for you and the world, offer a record of ancient history, or offer timeless wisdom and inspiration? Has your experience of reading the Bible been positive or negative, illuminating or confusing? You'll get more from your reading of this book, I think, if you briefly take stock of where you are at the outset of our journey together. So take just a couple of minutes. You can write some notes right here in the margins or in the space provided below.

Once you've done this, we're ready to get started. The Bible really is an amazing book. I'm very glad you've decided to venture into it one more time, and I'm grateful that you've invited me to come along.

Insights and Questions

- How would I describe the Bible?
- What has been my experience with the Bible?

CHAPTER 1

What Is the Bible?

Okay, so my first question is kind of basic, maybe even dumb.

There are no dumb questions.

Everyone says that.

I mean it. Really. A lot of people think they should know a lot about the Bible and are embarrassed they don't, so they never join others in talking about it or trying to understand it. They don't want to sound dumb, but then they never learn anything.

I often feel like that. I mean, I do know something about the Bible. I went to Sunday school as a kid . . . sometimes. But I don't remember much, and I don't feel like I know enough.

Don't worry about it. You aren't alone, and you probably know more than you think. Even if you don't, even if you know next to nothing, what's the big deal? You've got to start somewhere. I'm just glad you're curious. So, really, no dumb questions—go ahead.

Okay, here goes—what is the Bible, anyway?

A book.

Funny.

Well, it is.

Duh. I know it is. I was looking for a little more.

Funny you should mention it, but there is something more.

Go on . . .

We get our English word *Bible* from the Greek word *ta biblia.* That's actually a plural noun meaning "the books." See what I mean? You're getting a whole collection of books, a whole library, all under one cover and for one low price.

Great value.

Yeah, it is. But, seriously, it matters that the Bible is a collection of books.

Sorry. I still don't get it.

Well, think about books, about what they do.

They tell us about stuff, give us information.

Sometimes.

And they tell us stories.

Yeah, that too. And that's really important because people—all of us—tend to make sense of our lives through stories.

What do you mean?

I mean that we do almost everything through story—tell people about ourselves, learn about others, share our hopes and dreams, just about everything. For instance, try to think of anything major in your life, anything that really mattered, that you haven't shared with someone else in story.

That's hard to do. But I'm still not sure why this matters.

Let me give you an example. Like most kids, my kids love hearing stories. From Eric Carle's *Brown Bear, Brown Bear* to *Harry Potter,* we've been reading to them since before they could sit up.

You're a good parent.

Thanks, but that's not really the point. The point is, they grew up on stories. Now that they're reading, it's incredible how many stories they've been exposed to. Not surprisingly, they've started to use some of the characters and plot lines from books to make sense of things that are happening to them. I remember one spring after my daughter had read one of the *Little House* books where the Ingalls family can't afford any Christmas presents. Do you know the scene I'm talking about?

I don't think I read that one.

Well, you know the basic story of the pioneer family.

Sure.

Okay. Well, the scene I'm thinking of is a pretty sad one. Pa's had a tough autumn, with a poor harvest and not much game, so come winter there's no money to buy presents, and things are looking pretty dreary. But when the girls show up at church on Christmas Eve, there are presents waiting for them. Folks back East had sent them out so the pioneer children wouldn't go without Christmas presents. Well, my daughter thought that was so cool she decided that for her next birthday she'd ask her friends to bring a donation for hurricane victims instead of presents.

She's a good kid.

Thanks, she is a good kid. But that's not really the point either. It's more that stories are powerful. They shape the way we think about ourselves, our lives, and our world. Stories give us our identity.

Say a little more about that.

Let me try another example.

Like I said, my kids love stories. And the stories they love best aren't always even from books but are the stories we tell them about our family. You know, stories about their aunts and uncles and grandparents. Stories about the funny things they did when they were kids. The funny things we did when we were little.

One of their favorites is about when I was around six years old. My family and I were all out for ice cream, when out of the blue I took my dish of ice cream and stuffed it into my older sister's face.

Why did you do that?!

No idea. Just one of those impulses you get when you're a kid and you just do it.

I bet your sister was mad.

Furious. But I thought it was so funny I laughed my head off. I laughed so hard, in fact, that when my dad spanked me . . .

He *spanked* you?

Different time.

. . . Anyway, he spanked me and I didn't even notice because I was laughing so hard. And then he spanked me again and I *wasn't* laughing anymore. Well, my kids love that story because . . .

Because they've done dumb stuff and have gotten into trouble and it's nice to know their parents did the same kinds of things.

Exactly.

Yeah, I remember hearing stories like that when I was little.

Stories, especially family stories, tell us who we are.

Let me give you another example. When my parents were visiting last summer, my dad told my kids about when he was eight and his town was flooded. It was so bad, people had to get him and his parents out of the second story window of their house by boat. My dad remembers a man patrolling the flooded streets in a canoe and calling back to a rowboat, "Two big ones and one little one in this house! Two big ones and one little one!"

My kids love that story and have asked to hear it again a couple of times since. Part of the reason is just because hearing that story gives them a connection to their grandpa. He's 80 now, but this story helps them imagine him when he was just a kid, like them, and so it makes him seem more real. But it's more than that, too. One of the first times they asked to hear that story was when we went down to the basement this fall for a tornado warning. And it helped. It was like the story wasn't just about their grandpa anymore but about them, and about how even when disaster strikes, you'll still have your parents around you and it'll end up okay.

Good stories do that. They tell us who we are by telling us what family we're a part of, giving us a sense that we belong, that we're part of something bigger.

Okay, I get that, but let's get back to the Bible.

We haven't really left it. The stories of the Bible work the same way. They tell us about our ancestors, our parents and grandparents and aunts and uncles in the faith. It helps us feel closer to these people who lived so long ago. We have a sense of knowing them, of belonging to the same family. And when we hear their stories, about their struggles or the tough scrapes they were in, it gives us hope and courage that we'll make it just like they did.

I think I see what you mean. As you get to know the stories in the Bible, you start to see that they are like your own stories. I guess you kind of start to see how they can make sense in your own life, like your kids did with your dad's story of the flood.

Right.

But there's a problem.

What's that?

Well, the Bible's not exactly a story, not even a neat collection of little stories. I mean, I've tried to read it. Some of it is stories, but a lot of it is not. A lot of it is different, even a little weird. So what do you do with all this other stuff, like all the rules and poems and long lists of names and the like? This isn't like any story I grew up with.

That's a great point. There is all kinds of stuff in the Bible. Which is kind of like life too.

What do you mean?

Well, think about your life story, about all the things you know about yourself and your family. I mean, it's not just stories about my family that we share with our kids; it's other stuff too. Like pictures of relatives and even of ancestors. Or letters my wife saved that her mom wrote to her when she was studying abroad during college. Or this lantern I have from my grandfather, who was an engineer on the Pennsylvania Railroad and used to wave from the engines he drove. Or a quilt my grandmother made. I've even got some sermons my great-grandfather preached and part of a diary from my great-great-grandfather, who went West as a young preacher.

You've got a lot of preachers in your family?

Yeah, I do.

Sorry, go on.

No, that's okay, because that's part of our story too. My great-great-grandfather, in the part of the diary we have, made out this list of rules he intended to abide by now that he was traveling to the "wild West."

What were the rules?

Oh, things like reading the Bible every day, praying for his family, and making sure he took communion at least four times a year. It may seem kind of goofy to us now, but it's part of the story. And then there are all the traditions.

Traditions?

Yeah, like opening the doors of the Advent calendar in the weeks leading up to Christmas. Or having pork and sauerkraut for dinner each New Year's Day. Or rice and curry for family reunions.

Hold on. You had pork and sauerkraut at New Year's and rice and curry at family reunions?

Well, yeah. The pork and sauerkraut is a German tradition to bring luck at the start of a new year. I grew up in Pennsylvania, and everyone had that on New Year's. And my mom and all her siblings grew up in India, where my grandfather was a missionary, so we always had rice and curry when we all got together. And as we ate the rice and curry my aunts and uncles and mom would eventually get around to telling stories about their adventures growing up. It might sound a little weird, but as a kid it was really cool. The food, the traditions, the keepsakes, the stories—they all helped to tell us about who we are.

I know what you mean. We always ate a special meal that was passed down from our immigrant great-grandparents. It was just as much a part of Christmas as decorating the tree and singing carols.

Exactly. It's all part of the story that tells you who you are.

And when you think about it, it's not just family stuff we collect. When I was little, we had a framed replica of Thomas Jefferson's rules for living a good life. You know—don't put off to tomorrow what you can do today; when you're angry count to 10 before speaking; when you're really angry count to 100. . . .

I thought that was Ben Franklin.

Maybe. Our list credited Jefferson. Either way, I remember those things now, all these years later. We're not related to Jefferson—or Franklin—but they're part of our story too. And all this stuff works together to tell the story of who we are.

We all have these kinds of things. And not just families. Churches have stories like this, and small towns. Big cities do too. Think of all the stories connected with Chicago being called the "Windy City," or New York as the "Big Apple." Even whole countries make sense of their history and identity through stories. I mean, think of all the stories we have about the United States, from the story of the signing of the Declaration of Independence and Abe Lincoln's teaching himself to read to the first Thanksgiving and George Washington's boyhood fiasco with a certain cherry tree.

But that last one didn't happen.

Washington and the cherry tree?

Yeah. It was made up, kind of an American Aesop's Fable.

True enough. Odds are the first Thanksgiving wasn't exactly the way we picture it either. But both of these stories are still part of the American story and help us understand what it means to be an American.

Well, the Bible is like that too. It's a collection of stories, and letters, and rules for living in a new country, and favorite songs, and passed-down traditions and rituals, and all kinds of other stuff. Taken together, it forms a kind of tapestry with many, many different threads that, when taken together, tells us a huge story about who Christians are, about who we are.

It seems more like a patchwork quilt to me.

You know, you're right. A patchwork quilt is a much better image.

Thank you.

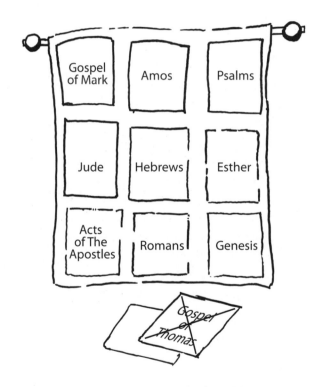

You're welcome.

That image really works. With a tapestry, there's usually one weaver and one design, all figured out ahead of time. A quilt might have one maker, too, but just as often groups of people gathered to work on their quilts together. And usually quilts were formed by pulling together all kinds of bits and pieces—some that might've been bought for the quilt, but usually the different pieces were scraps left over from old pants and jackets and blankets, brought together to make something new, something unique, something useful. And quilts often tell a story too: the pieces and where they came from, the way the pieces were fitted together—stars, circles, different shapes— not to mention the stitching patterns.

The other image that comes to mind is a scrapbook.

That one works, too, maybe even better. After all, a scrapbook is a kind of family album, a collection of all kinds of things that, taken together, tell the story of a particular person or family. In the case of the Bible, instead of it being pictures of the prom, birth certificates, and wedding bulletins, it's parables, psalms, and the letters of Paul. Same idea, though: all those bits and pieces, taken together, create a family scrapbook that tells the story of the people of God.

Okay, this is all very helpful. I am definitely getting a better sense of what the Bible is and how it all holds together.

Great.

But I've still got a major problem with all this.

What's that?

Well, it's this whole notion of "story." I mean, I get that stories are important, that they tell us who we are, and all. But . . . are you really saying the Bible is just a bunch of stories? Or even one big Story? Shouldn't it mean something more, something more powerful, something more . . . I don't know . . . just *more* . . .

Magical?

Sort of. I mean, not really magical, but something different, something more otherworldly, something more divine, I guess.

It's funny you should put it that way. I have a hunch that most people, including most church-going people, tend to think of the Bible as a kind of divine reference book.

Yes. Exactly. I think that's the way I grew up thinking about it too. The Bible is something with all the answers in it—answers from God, which is why it's special, different from other stories.

But think about it: in that very image is the problem with the way most of us were taught to think about the Bible.

How so?

Well, what does a reference book do? It essentially sits on the shelf until you need to look something up. And I think that's the way the Bible functions in a lot of homes. It basically sits on the shelf or cof-fee table, more like a decoration than something that has anything really useful to say.

That doesn't mean it has to work that way. I mean, we could read it every day. I know some people who do.

I know some people who do too. But most, at least most of the people I know, don't. It may have a lot of answers, but it doesn't seem that interesting to read, so most of us just don't.

I'm a little embarrassed to admit it, but I have to say that's how it works in our home. We don't really get it out to read that often.

Don't feel too bad. You're not alone. I bet you don't get out the dictionary or encyclopedia all that often, either.

Plus, even when we do read it more regularly, a lot of us don't find that it works all that well as an "answer book."

I have to agree. When I have read it, I'll admit that I found it a little hard to understand. There's a lot there that seems, well, just plain bizarre. Not to mention that a whole lot of things we have to deal with don't necessarily show up in the Bible—things like a concern for the environment or thoughts about nuclear war or how to raise your children in the changing world we live in with computers, iPods, and the rest.

You're not alone. Even many of us who read and study the Bible regularly have a hard time getting it to work like our other reference books, as if all the answers are just there waiting for you to look them up.

Lots of people seem to use it that way, though, quoting chapter and verse of this or that to tell me what to think, what to do, even how to vote.

How do you react to that?

I don't really buy it. I mean, it doesn't always feel like the little piece of the Bible being quoted matches the question we're talking about. But I don't feel like I know enough about the Bible to answer.

I understand what you mean. I think that's what is most helpful about thinking about the Bible as a collection of things that together tells us a huge Story about who we are. Like we said before, it's not exactly like the stories we grew up with. It's chock full of all kinds of different things, some that seem pretty odd to us. But all those bits and pieces collected together make up this huge scrapbook, and that scrapbook tells the story of God and the people of God.

So rather than give us once-and-for-all answers, the Bible invites us into a story, gives us an identity, and helps us figure out our questions on the basis of that story and identity. I mean, think about it—did anyone quote chapter and verse at you from your family scrapbook while you were growing up in order to teach you what it means to be a member of your family?

No. Not really.

My family didn't either. They told stories, kept traditions, looked at pictures, and over time all these things and more shaped your sense of your family and yourself. Out of this identity you've come to make all kinds of decisions or choices.

That makes sense. But I have to admit I'd still like something more than a "story."

I think you may be underestimating stories. Stories, at least the really big stories like we're talking about, don't just describe things.

They don't?

No. I mean, they are describing things. But at the same time they're also making claims.

Claims?

Yeah, about how life really is, about who God is and who we are. Ultimately, stories make claims about reality, about how things really are.

Think, again, about all the stories, traditions, celebrations, and the like that we have about our country. They don't just remind us of things or connect us with the Americans who came before or even give us our identity. They make claims about what America really is, about it being a special country, about it being blessed, about it having a unique place and role in the world.

Maybe. Although I'm guessing a lot of people in the world wouldn't agree with that.

Great point. Which just goes to show that there are other stories about reality that are out there, competing for our attention. Whether you agree with the claim or not is another matter. But make no mistake that the "American story" is making a claim, a big claim, about reality, about the way things really are.

The Bible does that too. Underneath all the various pieces of this quilt, beneath all the things we find in this scrapbook, is a Story that makes claims about the way the world really is, about the way God really is. And when you read it, you're invited to take those claims seriously and see whether they ring true for you, whether this Story can and should be your story.

Maybe. I'm not totally sure how that works. I mean, there are so many different stories in the big one. Can you give me an example?

How about two?

Even better.

Great. Let's start with King David; he's one of the most important characters in the Old Testament. And for good reason: he's strong, brave, loves God, defeats Israel's enemies, and more. But at the same time he's also this guy who steals another man's wife, has major problems with his kids, and regularly disappoints God and his people.

Then let's jump to the New Testament and Peter. He's one of Jesus' closest friends, the leader of the disciples, and the guy who first confesses that Jesus is the Messiah. Yet he's also the one who denies Jesus three times and deserts him when Jesus most needed him.

Sheesh, you really picked a couple of winners!

But that's just it. People like David and Peter —complicated people who do good things and bad things, who have great days and awful days, who sometimes win and sometimes lose—people like this are all over the Bible.

Sounds like people I know.

Exactly. And so from all these bits and pieces, from all these little stories, we get a part of the larger Story. The point is, God isn't looking for perfect people, but meets these very ordinary people—people, that is, who are a whole lot like us—just where they are. And as we read these stories, we realize the same thing is true for us: even though we're ordinary, even complicated people, God's willing to meet us where we are, and, if we're willing, God can do great things through us.

And that's what you mean by saying that the Bible is making a claim? That it's trying to be our story?

Right. That's why all these different pieces were collected together over time, because all the things in the Bible—the stories and rituals and songs and rules—together paint a picture of a particular kind of reality that is different from the reality another religion with a different set of scriptures would paint.

That makes sense. The Bible is like the Christian family scrapbook that offers a Christian version of the way the world really is.

Right.

But there's still a major problem.

What's that?

It's right there in your example with David and Peter. I mean, it seems like there's not just *one* story in the Bible. What about the Old Testament, where we hear about David, and the New Testament, where we meet Peter? It really seems like they're part of two different stories.

In what way?

Well, isn't the Old Testament kind of like a Jewish version of the Story, and the New Testament is a Christian version?

I can see what you mean. Maybe it will help if we think about the Old and New Testaments as two parts to a larger story, rather than as two separate stories.

But they really *are* different. I remember enough from Sunday school to know that. I mean, they've even got totally different main characters, with the people of Israel starring in the first story and Jesus taking up most of the second.

That's a good point. But what if the main character isn't either Israel or Jesus?

Well, I'm willing to hear you out. But I'll be honest, I'm a little skeptical.

That's okay; a little skepticism can be a good thing.

Good, because it's hard to see how the Israelites aren't the main character of the Old Testament. Okay, so you start with Adam and Eve, but pretty soon you're on to Abraham, Moses, and all the kings and prophets.

True enough.

And, quite frankly, I don't think you should say Jesus isn't what the New Testament's about. Couldn't that get you into trouble?

I suppose it could, but I'll take that risk.

Seriously, though, certainly Israel is a main character. And so is Jesus. He's got four Gospels totally devoted to him. And then the church becomes a major character too.

I hadn't thought of that.

After the Gospels comes the Acts of the Apostles, the story of the founding of the church, and then all the letters that are also about the life of the early church. Even so, what if the central character isn't Israel, Jesus, or the church?

Then who's it about?

God.

God?

Yeah, God. I think that's what holds the two parts of the Bible together. The Bible is first and foremost a collection of books that tell the story of God.

The God who creates the world and all the plants, animals, and people in it.

The God who wants to be in relationship with humanity and so sets apart one particular group of people to bless and through them to bless the whole world.

The God who puts up with the complaints, the disobedience, the lack of faith of this people, sending them prophet after prophet to draw them back into relationship.

The God who finally becomes one of these people, becomes human, by sending his Son Jesus to tell them of God's love.

The God who raises that Son from death when he is rejected and crucified.

The God who gathers the church to tell the world about Jesus and his resurrection and about the love of God these things signify.

The God, finally, who promises to come again to bring an end to war and division, even creating a new heaven and new earth.

That's quite a story.

Yes, it is, but what else could you expect from a story about God? And that's what the Bible is ultimately about—God. It does have two major parts, but it's one story, the story of God and God's unyielding, tenacious, and indefatigable desire to love, bless, and save the whole world.

"Unyielding, tenacious, indefatigable." Those are big words. I'm not even sure I know what the last one means.

It means "tireless." Yes, they are big words, but they're good adjectives to describe God as the main character in the Bible. Because in the biblical story, God will do just about anything to tell the world and everyone in it that they are loved, that they have value, that they are special to God, and that God has a place and purpose for them.

I like that.

I do too. But it gets even better. 'Cause there's another character we haven't even talked about, yet.

Really? Who?

Us.

Us?

Yeah, us. That's the whole point. It's the story, as I said, of God *and* the people of God. That's where we come in. We're part of the people of God. So the Bible is our story.

Maybe. Except that the people in the Bible lived thousands of years ago. The stuff God did and said was for them, not us.

That's not the way stories work, though. Stories—at least the big stories, the ones that matter—whether they're set in the past or even the future, are always really about the present.

Wait a minute. Why are the big stories *always* about the present?

Think of it this way. We study history, not just out of an interest in the past but to make sense of our present. When you read Lincoln's Gettysburg Address or listen to King's "I Have a Dream" speech, you're not only, or even primarily, interested in the past; you're interested in what that past event tells you about the present, about what it means to be alive now.

Yeah, I guess that's true.

And sometimes it's even more obvious, like when a writer sets a book or play in the past to make a point about the present.

Okay. I get that. I remember hearing that about Arthur Miller's play called *The Crucible*. It was set in the time of the Salem witch trials, but was really about what Joseph McCarthy was doing in the 1950s with the "red scare."

Right. That's a really good example. And now, of course, when someone like George Clooney makes a movie about the 1950s, like he did in *Good Night, and Good Luck*, the story of Edward R. Murrow's attempt to expose McCarthy, that's not just about the 1950s—it's also about our own time, our own government.

Interesting. So whether we hear a story that is actual history or simply set in history, we're always thinking about the present.

Right, and who can blame us, since we don't live in the past or future but right smack dab in the middle of the present.

That makes sense. And you think that's what's going on in the Bible?

Absolutely. At some places, you can even see this at work.

What do you mean?

Well, take the story of the Ten Commandments.

You mean like from the Charlton Heston movie?

Sort of. The movie is definitely based on the Bible, but . . .

I know, I know, you're going to tell me the book is way better.

It is. But I was actually going to say that in the Bible, there are two accounts of God giving the Ten Commandments.

Really? I didn't know that. Why does it have that story twice?

The first time is in the book of Exodus, and it's the story we all know. The second time is in the book of Deuteronomy, and it's set 40 years later. Except for Moses and two other guys, everyone who was there when God gave the Ten Commandments has died. So the people of Israel are about to enter into the promised land, and Moses reminds them of when God gave them the law at Mount Sinai, the law they're supposed to live by once they're in the new land.

So it's like a flashback.

Yeah, except when Moses tells them the story, he doesn't make it about the past. Instead, he sets it in the present. Here, I'll read it for you; it's in the fifth chapter:

> *The Lord our God made a covenant with us at Horeb . . .*

Sorry, "Horeb"?

It's another name for Mount Sinai.

Thanks. Go ahead.

Okay.

> *The Lord our God made a covenant with us at Horeb. Not with our ancestors did the Lord make this covenant, but with us, who are all of us here alive today. The Lord spoke with you face to face at the mountain, out of the fire. (At that time I was standing between the Lord and you to declare to you the words of the Lord; for you were afraid because of the fire and did not go up the mountain.) (Deuteronomy 5:2-5)*

Wait a second. I thought you said just about everyone was dead.

They are.

But then he's not exactly telling the truth. In fact, it seems like he's going out of his way to change the facts.

If you're talking about what actually happened, you're right. But I think there's something else going on here. Moses is saying that, for all intents and purposes, the people coming into the promised land *are* God's people, the people God rescued from Egypt, the people God gave the law. There is no other Israel. They are now the ones in relationship with God, the ones to whom God has promised to be faithful. That's why he goes out of his way to say "not with your ancestors, but with *us*, all of *us* who are alive here *today*." By retelling this story, Moses is pulling these new people into that story, making it their own.

Okay, I think I get what you're saying. When we tell and hear the biblical story, it becomes our story, just like the story of the Ten Commandments was the story of the Israelites who came generations after God actually gave the Ten Commandments.

Exactly. But there's something more too. And I'm going to warn you ahead of time, what I want to explain is going to sound ridiculously simple, but I still think it's really cool.

Okay . . .

Well, think about where the Bible begins.

Genesis?

Right, which means "beginning." So the Bible begins at the very beginning, with the creation of the world. And it ends . . .

In Revelation.

Right. At the very end.

You're right. That does sound pretty simple.

I know, but here's the cool part. The Bible begins at the very beginning and ends at the very end. But we're not at the end yet. We're actually living somewhere between the Acts of the Apostles and Revelation. And so we're main characters, too, taking our part in the unfolding biblical drama that starts in the beginning and won't end till the very end.

Kinda cool, isn't it?

Yeah, it is. Although it's going to take a little while to sink in.

That's okay. It's kind of incredible.

At some points you can almost feel the biblical story opening up to include us. There's a part in John's Gospel where Jesus prays for the disciples. And all of a sudden, he says that he's praying not only for his disciples but for all those who will come to believe because of them (see John 17:20). Well, guess what: we're part of the ones who come to believe because of the disciples. We're some of those Jesus is praying for.

That is cool.

Or think about near the end of the Gospel of John when Jesus is talking to Thomas.

Doubting Thomas?

Just the one. The line I'm thinking about comes just after Thomas got to see Jesus and stopped doubting. He says to Thomas, "Have you believed because you have seen me? Blessed are those who have not seen and yet have come to believe" (John 20:29). Again, we're part of those who haven't seen Jesus and still believe. So he's actually blessing us.

Again, very cool.

I think so too.

So the Bible is a book . . . well, a collection of books, made up of all different parts and pieces like a patchwork quilt or family scrapbook.

Right.

And it tells the story of God and the people of God, from the Israelites through Jesus and the church and right up to us.

Yes. And through this story the Bible is making a claim about the way things really are, and it is inviting us into that story, to make it our own and take our place in it.

Okay. That makes sense to me. But I've still got some more questions.

That's okay. I've got time.

Insights and Questions

CHAPTER 2

Is the Bible True?

Alright, so something's been bugging me since you mentioned Washington.

Washington?

Yeah, George Washington and the cherry tree. About how it doesn't matter that it never happened because it's still part of our story.

Go ahead.

Well, this is a tough one. Are you sure you won't get annoyed?

Definitely. Asking tough questions is part of what being faithful is all about.

Seriously?

Seriously. Read the book of Job sometime, or the Psalms. They're chock full of tough questions people ask about God or even ask God directly.

Okay, I will. But not right now. For now, I want to know if you think the Bible's true.

... Uh oh. You're not saying anything. I hope you're not offended.

No, I'm not. I'm just thinking. It's a very good question.

Really?

Yeah, it's an important question to talk about.

Thanks. I thought so too. I mean, it's one thing to say that George Washington didn't cut down the cherry tree—and it's no big deal. It's another to say that maybe some things the Bible describes didn't happen.

You're right, this is important stuff. Okay, first let me give you the simple answer. Yes, I think the Bible's true—I believe that absolutely, definitively, and without reservation.

I thought so. I mean you talked about it as a collection of stories that tell the truth about God, about our lives, and about the world we live in.

I'm impressed—you were really listening.

Yeah, I was. But what I don't understand is how you can also compare the stories in the Bible to some of the stories we know aren't true, like Washington and the cherry tree.

I see what you mean. I do think the Bible is true. But that's not the same thing as saying everything in the Bible happened just the way it was described. Jonah and the whale. Joshua stopping the sun in its tracks. The world being created in six days. I'm not at all convinced these things happened just as they're described in the Bible.

To tell you the truth, I sorta feel the same way. But then, how can the Bible be true?
Gosh, when I think about these things, I often feel a little guilty. Like if I was more faithful, I'd believe everything just as it happened. And I do believe a lot of it happened, but some things don't seem, I don't know, believable.

Plus, I'm never totally sure what to make of the people who seem to think it all happened just like the Bible says. You know, the people who fight about teaching the creation story as science in the public schools. I mean, they're Christian, but I just can't make myself think this way. Does that mean I'm a bad Christian?

No, it definitely doesn't. Like I said earlier, asking questions isn't wrong. In fact, I think it's a sign of faith.

At the same time, you're absolutely right, this is a big question, a huge question, actually.

I thought so too. 'Cause it feels like there are only two options: either the Bible is telling the truth, and I have to believe some things I have a hard time swallowing, or the Bible's not telling the truth, and then I have to wonder why we're reading it at all.

I think you've hit the nail right on the head. It does feel like there are only two options. And that makes sense when you're thinking about the Bible as a divine reference book. After all, who would use a dictionary that misspelled some of the words or an encyclopedia that got some of its facts wrong?

Exactly. So which is it?

The thing is, I don't think those are our only two options.

The question we need to ask, I think, isn't *whether* the Bible is true. As I already said, I definitely believe it is. Instead, the question is *how* the Bible is true. And that's a huge question that will take a little time to unpack. So let me get at it by asking you a question.

Okay.

When you ask if the Bible is "true," what do you mean? To put it another way: what makes something true?

Well, you know—if it really happened.

Thanks. I think that's a good answer, one a lot of us would offer. So it sounds like we're talking mainly about truth as accurate facts, things we can prove, like the date the Revolutionary War ended or that 2+2=4.

Yeah. I think you could say that.

Are there any things that are true that aren't facts?

What do you mean?

Well, I'm totally with you that when we're dealing with facts, we talk about truth in terms of accuracy. Facts can be proven to be true or false.

Right.

But I think there are other things that we believe are true and that make a big difference in our lives because we believe they are true, and yet we can't prove them.

Like what?

Well, what about freedom?

What *about* freedom?

Well, do you believe that people are better off when they are free or when they are slaves?

Free, of course.

So you are absolutely against slavery?

Absolutely.

I believe that too. People haven't always thought that way, of course.

Maybe not, but they were wrong.

I agree. But there have been any number of times in human history when people believed freedom was not that important—that it was okay, even right, to keep some people as slaves.

Like I said, they were wrong. Slavery is just plain wrong and it always has been, even if people didn't think so. Freedom is something everyone deserves. It's right there in the Declaration of Independence: "life, liberty, and the pursuit of happiness."

You've got some strong feelings about this. I mean, you sound really convinced that this is true.

Of course I am! Come on, we fought a war about this.

Again, I totally agree. But here's the thing: prove it.

What?

Prove to me that slavery is wrong.

It just is. Can't you see that?

Yes, I do, but I still want you to prove it.

But this isn't something you should have to prove. Slavery is just plain wrong. Like they say in the Declaration of Independence, it's just self-evident. You know, "We hold these truths to be self-evident, that all men are created equal, that they are endowed by their Creator with certain unalienable rights, that among these are life, liberty, and the pursuit of happiness."

Wow. You've got a good memory.

Thanks. I had a great seventh-grade history teacher. Look, I know you believe this too. So what's the point?

The point is that you're right: we all believe that some things shouldn't have to be proved. We know they're just right. But, the thing is, it's not just that they shouldn't have to be proved; it's also that they can't be proved, at least not in the same way.

What do you mean?

I mean, there is fundamentally no way to prove that freedom is better than slavery. You can give all kinds of good reasons. But, ultimately, it's not a matter of facts; it's a matter of beliefs, of convictions, of values. That doesn't make it any less true, or any less important. When you think about it, most of the really, really important things in life are like this.

Say a little more.

Freedom is just one example of something that is incredibly important to us but that we can't reduce to facts to prove or disprove. The same is true with a lot of the huge beliefs we believe are just plain true. In addition to freedom, we also value love, life, faithfulness, and so on. But there's no way to prove that love is better than hate or indifference, that life is better than death, or that being faithful to someone is better than betraying them. In fact, there have been particular cultures that have believed very differently than we do today about each of these matters. And yet, these are things we believe to be true, and they also are really, really important to us. I sort of think that's what we mean when we say something is "self-evident"—that we believe it's so important and so true that we shouldn't have to prove it because it's a given, obvious, just plain right.

I see what you mean. But what happens to facts?

Facts are really important and obviously have a lot to do with truth. But they're not the only way to talk about truth, and taken by themselves they rarely offer a complete picture of truth, at least about the kinds of truth that matter most to us.

How do you mean?

Well, think about when you are first getting to know someone. Actually, let's make it a little more interesting and call it a first date.

Okay.

Unless it's a blind date, you usually know the person you're going out with at least a little bit, and sometimes more than a little bit. But this is still a whole new level of relationship, so you're very interested in getting to know the person you're going out with a whole lot better.

Absolutely.

So what do you do?

What do you mean?

How do you get to know the person you're dating better? How do you get some sense of the truth about who that person really is and the potential this relationship holds?

You ask some questions.

Fact questions?

What?

Do you ask them for facts about themselves? Age, what kind of job they have, what their favorite color is, how much they weigh.

How much they weigh?! Are you kidding? Not unless you want this date over in a hurry!

Actually I was kidding about that part. What I'm really interested in is whether you get to know someone primarily through information, through facts.

Well, you usually do want some information, and so you might ask a few questions. But mostly you tell each other about yourself.

And you do that with . . . ?

Okay, I get it. Yes, you usually do that with stories. One person starts and before long it's, "Oh, that reminds me of . . ." and "I remember the time . . ."

Exactly. As we talked about earlier, most of what matters to us we share through story. There's a kind of narrative truth about who we are and what we believe that's at least as important as the facts we share.

But you can't prove this kind of truth.

Well, over time you can *experience* the truth of what you believe. Like whether the person you get to know really is like he or she told you on that first date, or whether freedom, love, and faithfulness really are better than their opposites. But, yes, you're right, you can't prove these things like you can a scientific hypothesis. Some truth claims you can prove; some you can't, but both are claims about truth.

I see what you mean. Actually, it makes a lot of sense. But it's hard not to think of truth in terms of facts.

Definitely. Facts are clearly very important in our lives. My point is that they aren't the only kind of truths that matter to us.

But you're absolutely right. We've been thinking about truth primarily in terms of facts for nearly 300 years.

What do you mean, 300 years? Haven't we always thought about truth this way?

No, not really. The fact-value split started getting popular around the early 1700s.

The "fact-value split"? Sounds like a complicated gymnastics routine.

It is complicated, though you'll never see it performed in the Olympics. Do you mind if I go into a little history to explain it?

No problem. Like I said, I had a great seventh-grade history teacher and enjoy history.

Great. Okay, so do you know much about the Thirty Year's War?

I'm guessing it lasted about 30 years. But seriously, not that much. We focused mainly on American history in seventh grade.

No problem. Essentially, a little less than a century after the Protestant Reformation, from 1618 to 1648, Europe went to war along political and religious lines, and it was awful. I mean, really, really bad, lasting—you guessed it—30 years. Between the battles, famine, and disease, Europe was devastated by the time it was over.

Well, in the years that followed, the survivors placed a lot of the blame for the war at the door of religious dogma.

Sounds like they were pretty hostile to religion.

As it turns out, most were Christians. It wasn't religious faith they were against. Rather, they opposed using religious dogma to settle political, social, and economic problems.

For example, they argued that one shouldn't try to figure out how the creation works primarily by speculating about the creator. Instead, they thought that you should use the intelligence the creator gave you to understand the creation.

Makes sense to me.

Yeah, in many ways it does. So rather than try to understand and order the natural world by relying on theology and revelation, they turned instead to human reason and experimentation. This was eventually called the Enlightenment, and it led to the development of the scientific method, among other things.

And this is where the issue of truth comes in?

Yup. Philosophers began to distinguish between the things we can know for certain and prove or disprove—facts—and those things that can't be proved and so can only be a matter of opinion—values.

Ah, so this is the fact-value split.

Exactly. Although in the beginning no one thought that truth only lived on one side of the equation. Instead, it's different kinds of truths. Pretty soon, though, especially as science grew and developed and began to dominate how we think, truth got pretty much equated with fact.

But how did people think about truth before the fact-value split?

Interesting question. For the most part, there were two main criteria for something to be considered true. First, it had to be logically consistent. You know, your argument had to hold together. There couldn't be any logical holes in what you were saying. To give you an example, the ancient Greek philosopher Socrates made a living from going around debating with people and pointing out the logical inconsistencies of their beliefs.

Sounds a little like he would have done well in politics today.

Probably so.

But I see what you are getting at. Things ought to line up. What's the second criterion?

Fidelity to the tradition. In essence, what you say is true can't contradict what people have known is true for centuries.

PRE-ENLIGHTENMENT

Truth =

Logical consistency
+
Fidelity to tradition

POST-ENLIGHTENMENT

Truth =

Logical consistency
+
Rational verifiability

Seriously? But how could you ever do or think anything new?

The goal wasn't to do something new, at least not totally new. If you wanted to argue for something innovative, you had to show that it really did line up with the traditions everyone already knew were true. So, for example, when Martin Luther and others were trying to get the Reformation going, they would always point out how what they were saying was supported in Scripture and by the ancient church. It was kinda like saying, "Hey, we're just going back to the way it used to be; it's the other guys who innovated."

So, I guess if you were a marketing agent in the ancient world, you wouldn't exactly be advertising your product as "new and improved."

Definitely not. "Tried and true" would probably sell better.

No wonder the Enlightenment shook things up.

Absolutely. The architects of the Enlightenment obviously kept the first criterion of logical consistency, but they totally rejected the issue of fidelity to tradition, substituting instead the criterion we still use today: rational verifiability—the ability to prove a theory with an experiment that can be replicated at any time and any place with the same results.

So in the ancient world, you didn't try to prove things?

Not quite. You tried to prove things. And some people, like Aristotle, even did experiments of a kind. But for the most part, the way you proved something was less about experiments and more about argumentation and persuasion. That is, it was your job to convince people by philosophy or theology that what you said made sense, that it matched or explained their experience, and that it lined up with the received tradition. If you could do that, then you had "proved" it was true.

Which is what the Enlightenment attacked?

Exactly. The Enlightenment thinkers made a clear division between what you *know*—and can prove through rational means—and what you only *believe*—and cannot prove. Another way to put it is the difference between *what is*—verifiable knowledge available to everyone—and *what ought to be*—convictions about how things should be.

FACT	VALUE
What you know . . . and can prove	What you believe . . . and cannot prove
What is = knowledge	*What ought to be* = convictions

And that's the fact-value split?

That's it. Which brings us back to the Bible.

Really?

Yeah. Let's go to the story of Jesus and Thomas again, just near the end of John's Gospel.

Yeah, I was actually thinking about that. Because Thomas asks for proof, doesn't he?

Interestingly, he does. He wants to see Jesus' wounds before he'll believe the news that Jesus has been raised from the dead.

I totally get that. It's like someone who's been diagnosed with a terminal illness and then is told of a new miracle cure. I mean, you want to believe it and everything, but you don't want to get your hopes up only to have them dashed again. We've all been taught somewhere along the way that if it sounds too good to be true, it probably is.

That's right. Thomas has gotten something of a bad rap over the years. I don't think the problem was his lack of faith; it's more that he was a realist.

Earlier in the Gospel, in chapter 11, he was the one who urged the other disciples to go with Jesus to Jerusalem so that they could die with him, if necessary. So he's definitely not a coward. He saw what was coming and was ready to meet it. But now, when suddenly people are saying Jesus—his friend and Lord whom he saw nailed to a cross and die—is alive, he just can't buy it. He wants proof.

And Jesus gives it to him, right?

> Well, yes and no. Jesus definitely invites him to come and touch his wounds, but when the moment arrives, Thomas doesn't need to anymore.

Well, I can see that. If I saw Jesus standing there, I wouldn't need to either.

> Absolutely. But then Jesus goes on to say that while Thomas believed because he saw, others would come to believe even though they haven't had a chance to see.

Yeah, I remember that. We talked about that earlier. Jesus even calls them "blessed" and, in a sense, blesses us because we're among those who believe even though we haven't seen.
> **You know, I always felt a little sorry for Thomas at that moment.**

> Really? How come?

Well, it's almost like Jesus is scolding him. But, gosh, the other disciples saw Jesus, too, and it's not like every one of us wouldn't like a little tangible evidence.

> I see what you mean. Yes, it's definitely harder to believe without seeing, without proof. But, when you think about it, that's essentially what faith is. It doesn't take much faith to believe that 2+2=4. In fact, you don't really have to have faith in any of the things that you've got proof for. Faith, according to the Letter to the Hebrews, is precisely "the assurance of things hoped for, the conviction of things not seen" (11:1). Which means that faith always fills in the gap between what we can see and prove and what we hope and believe is true.

Which is why faith is hard. There is always an element of uncertainty.

> Yes, and I think the writers of the Bible knew that too. I think that's why John includes Jesus' blessing of those who believe without seeing. I don't think he's scolding Thomas as much as he is pointing out the limitations of proof. I mean, when Thomas sees Jesus, he doesn't just agree that Jesus has been raised from the dead—he goes on to make this incredible confession, calling Jesus "my Lord and my God." No one else in any of the Gospels calls Jesus "God," but Thomas does.

And while touching Jesus' wounds might "prove" that it's really Jesus standing in front of him, it doesn't prove that he's God. So even proof can only go so far; at some point faith has to take over.

I'm not sure I'm following.

Facts can tell what something *is*, but they can't tell you what that thing *means*. So while you might be able to prove what sequence of historical events led to the Civil War, you definitely can't prove what the Civil War means. In the same way, seeing Jesus may prove to Thomas that Jesus is alive, but it doesn't prove what that means. And so Thomas has to make a confession of faith about what it means to him. It's not something Thomas can prove, but it's definitely something he believes, and it's definitely something that shapes the rest of his life.

Which is why, I think, the Bible was written.

How do you mean?

Let's read the next two verses in John after the scene with Thomas: "Now Jesus did many other signs in the presence of his disciples, which are not written in this book. But these are written so that you may come to believe that Jesus is the Messiah, the Son of God, and that through believing you may have life in his name" (John 20:30-31).

Keeping in mind that these are some of the last verses in John's Gospel, what do you make of what he says here?

It's almost like John is coming clean on what he's been up to all along.

How so? .

Well, he says that there are a lot of other things he could have written, but he didn't. So he's making choices. And he's based his choices on what he thinks will convince us that Jesus is the Messiah. I think it's like you said: he's trying to persuade his readers—and I guess that includes us—that his story of Jesus is true. He can't offer us scientific proof, but he can tell us this story.

Which is why I think it matters that these verses come right after the scene with Thomas.

That makes sense. Number one: Thomas has just made a confession of faith that John hopes we'll make. Number two: Jesus blesses those who don't have the advantage the disciples have and so encourages us to believe without seeing.

Nicely put.

Thanks. But, you know, I still kind of wish there was proof.

I know what you mean. We live in a post-Enlightenment world where rational proof is highly valued. And so it feels like it would be a little easier if we could prove things in the Bible like we can prove how the light bulb works. Which might be why so many people treat the Bible like a divine reference book, reading it like it's a book of facts instead of a book of faith.

Because facts are easier than faith?

I think so.

You know, that's interesting. I never thought of that before. I couldn't really understand why people got so worked up about teaching creation instead of evolution in schools, but if your only sense of truth is factual accuracy, I can suddenly see why proving all the "facts" of the Bible becomes important.

Exactly. Which means that if you operate with a fact-equals-truth sense of the Bible, you keep pretty busy.

How so?

Well, there are just tons of things that don't line up in the Gospels alone, let alone the rest of the Bible.

Like what?

Well, some of the inconsistencies are pretty small. Like how in Matthew and Mark, the disciples fall asleep three times while Jesus is praying the Garden of Gethsemane, and in Luke it's only once. Or in Mark, Jesus tells Peter he'll deny Jesus three times before the cock crows twice and, indeed, Peter denies Jesus once and the cock crows, and he denies Jesus two more times, and the cock crows a second time. But in Matthew, Luke, and John, Peter denies Jesus three times before the cock crows, just as Jesus foretold.

Seems like it could have been an innocent mistake.

It certainly could have been. But, innocent or not, if your sense of truth is limited to factual accuracy, you've got a problem.

Yeah, I can see that.

Then there is the issue of what I call "rearranged scenes."

What do you mean?

Sometimes the same scene appears at different places in the different Gospels. Like the scene of Jesus' clearing the temple of the money changers. In Matthew, Mark, and Luke, that happens near the end of Jesus' ministry, just after he enters Jerusalem and the week before he is crucified. In John, however, it happens right in the beginning of his public ministry.

So . . . could it be that he ran people out of the temple twice?

That's what folks defending the "factual accuracy" of the Bible in fact contend. And in fact it is possible. But then you have a story of Jesus' ministry that none of the Gospels reported.

What do you mean?

I mean simply that none of the Gospel writers tell a story in which Jesus chases the money changers out of the temple twice. So now you've got a version of the story that isn't faithful to any of them.

Interesting. And you said these are examples of minor discrepancies. What's an example of a larger one?

How 'bout disagreeing on when Jesus died?

Are you kidding me?

No. In all the Gospels, Jesus dies . . . when?

Friday, of course; that's why we call it Good Friday.

Right. And in Matthew, Mark, and Luke, this is the day of the Jewish festival of Passover. But in John, it's the day before Passover.

That's odd. It seems like that would be one detail they'd want to agree on. I mean, if Lincoln were shot on Christmas Day, I don't think we'd have some

folks arguing that it was really Christmas Eve. Some facts don't seem that hard to keep straight.

True. Unless, of course, you're not particularly interested in facts.

What do you mean?

John is telling a story that is meant to convince us of the truth of who and what Jesus is, and to do that he isn't relying only on facts but on a narrative. From early on in the Gospel, one of the themes John has been developing is that Jesus is like the Passover lamb whose death takes away the sin of the people. That's what John the Baptist says, in fact, when he first sees Jesus—although only in John's Gospel. So it makes sense that in John's account, Jesus dies not on Passover but on the Day of Preparation, the day before Passover, because that's when the Passover lamb is sacrificed.

So did Jesus die on Passover or not?

I don't know.

Don't you think that's a problem?

Only if what's most important about Jesus' death is *when* it happened. You know, getting the facts straight. I think the Gospel writers were more interested in *why* Jesus died—that is, what his death meant and, even more, what it might still mean to us.

Ah, I see. John is making a point.

A very important point about the truth of Jesus and the significance of his death—a truth that is so much bigger than the fact of whether Jesus died on Passover or the day before.

So what some might call a discrepancy or a mistake is actually an important detail in the different story the writer is telling.

Exactly. Often these details give you clues to the very truth the evangelist is trying to convey.

What about the different number of times the disciples fall asleep, one or three?

It's important to Mark's story that no one, even the disciples, understands who Jesus is until he dies on the cross. Even the disciples regularly misunderstand what Jesus is saying or fall short of expectations, including falling asleep three times. Luke, on the other hand, has a more compassionate view of the disciples and so only reports them falling asleep once. He even adds that they fell asleep "because of grief" (Luke 22:45), which neither Mark nor Matthew tell.

Interesting. And the rearranging of the scene with Jesus chasing the money changers out of the temple?

In Matthew, Mark, and Luke, this is kind of "the straw the broke the camel's back." Jesus has come right onto the central turf of the religious authorities and disrupted everything. It's right after this, in fact, that the Pharisees plot to have Jesus killed.

And in John?

Remember again that one of John's themes is that Jesus is the Passover lamb. For this reason, very early in Jesus' ministry, John describes Jesus disrupting the sacrificial system of the temple because he, Jesus, is God's own sacrifice to take away the sin of the world, and so there is simply no more *need* for temple sacrifice.

Again, it seems like John is making a point that we'd miss if we mushed all the "differences" together. It's really quite fascinating.

Yeah, it is. As John says near the end of his Gospel, he's making choices in order that his story will be compelling, and I think that's true of all the Gospel writers.

But what do you do if you're convinced that, in order to prove the truth of the Bible, it has to be factually accurate?

Well, you've got problems, small problems with small discrepancies, big problems with big ones. When push comes to shove, though, you can usually explain away almost any inconsistency if you try hard enough. One of the more popular books that does just that actually runs nearly 500 pages.

You can't be serious!

And another one tops 600.

All this to defend the belief that truth has to equal factual accuracy?

Well, to be fair, they believe they're defending the Bible, and because they believe that only verifiable facts can be accepted as truth, they have to make sure that every detail in Scripture is consistent.

That's true. But if you look at just the example from John, about what day Jesus dies, it seems as if the biblical writers themselves didn't understand truth that way.

You're right; they didn't. They definitely thought that what they believed was true. But they just didn't equate truth with facts. That notion comes after the Enlightenment.

For the biblical writers, truth was bigger than facts. And so instead of offering some kind of scientific proof, they told a story about God and Jesus and invited people into the story, invited people to make sense of their lives on the terms of this story.

And you know what? That's what the church has been doing for most of its history. I mean, almost no one until fairly recently thought we should read the Bible like a reference book filled with facts.

That's weird. To hear people talk about it, you'd think reading the Bible literally—you know, treating it like a book of facts—is the original and only way to read it.

I know, but it's not. Reading the Bible literally is pretty much an invention of the twentieth century, a reaction to the fact-value split we were talking about earlier. Once people started equating truth with fact, then some people thought that if the Bible was going to be seen as true, you had to defend its factual accuracy. So, their only choices are the ones you named earlier: either "all the accounts in the Bible are factually accurate and the Bible is true" or "some of the accounts in the Bible aren't factually accurate and so the Bible is false."

Once you put it like that, the choice seems pretty easy. No wonder you get books by certain Christians defending creation in seven days and so forth.

The interesting thing is, though, that prior to the Enlightenment, this wasn't a problem. For instance, do you know much about St. Augustine?

Not much. Only that he's pretty famous. People still quote him.

Yes, we do. Augustine lived around 400 A.D., was a bishop, and wrote some of the most influential books in the church's history. Many consider him the greatest theologian of the first thousand years of the church's history. But did you know he wasn't a Christian until later in life?

I didn't.

Yeah. He was a teacher of rhetoric, was pretty well-known in his social circles, had a mistress, and for many years didn't really want to become a Christian.

Sounds like he had an interesting life, to say the least.

He really did. You can read all about it in a book he called his *Confessions*. It's still widely read.

But what I really wanted to say was that one of the reasons he didn't want to become a Christian was because he thought Christians expected you to read the Bible literally, and he just couldn't do it.

You're kidding.

No. He read stories like Jonah in the whale and thought that if Christians believed this really happened as the story says, he didn't want to be a part of their religion. And then he met a guy named Ambrose, who was the bishop of Milan, who told him that, no, Christians don't read the Bible literally. Christians, as Ambrose explained to Augustine, see in these and other stories a greater truth about God as the creator of the cosmos and everything in it—the creation stories—or about God's concern for all the nations, even those who are Israel's enemies. That's what the book of Jonah's about.

I like that. I mean, I agree with Augustine. I don't think I could read the Bible literally. It just feels like I have to stop thinking at too many points. It helps to think about truth differently, that there's a bigger truth out there that can't be reduced to mere facts.

I think so too. But there's another reason why it's important to recognize that the biblical writers were trying to persuade us of the truth they offered rather than prove it to us.

What's that?

Well, think about it: how much emotional connection do you have to facts?

What do you mean?

I mean, how much do you, yourself, get involved in believing facts? What's at stake for you?

What do you mean, "believing facts"? Facts don't need belief. They just are. That's kind of what we've been talking about, isn't it?

Yes, it is.

Then I think I see your point. I mean, I might believe one political candidate is better than the other, and I can provide all kinds of good reasons, but when I talk with a friend of mine who disagrees with me, it's not like I can prove it. It's kind of a matter of faith. Like you said, 2+2=4 doesn't take faith, but beliefs that matter, but that you can't prove, do.

I agree. Facts don't require any personal investment. There's nothing of you particularly at stake. I mean, if you find out a fact you believe is wrong, that can shake things up, but for the most part we cruise along assuming our facts are, well, factual and don't think or even care about them much.

When it comes to faith, though, you're very much invested. So by offering us stories that require faith instead of facts, the Bible is making a claim on our whole selves, our whole lives. John doesn't pretend to write a neutral account of Jesus. He's after something; namely, he's after us and our faith. And so he tells a story big enough that, once we're done reading it, we might join Thomas in this incredible confession of faith.

I never thought of it that way. It's like faith makes a bigger invitation. I mean, for facts you only need your mind. You agree or you don't. But with faith you definitely use your mind, too, but you also need your heart and your imagination as well.

That's a great way to put it.

Plus, making it a matter of faith respects me as a person more, too.

How do you mean?

Well, with facts, it's really easy to assume you're just right, and anyone who doesn't agree with you is just wrong. You'd have to be an idiot to not agree that 2+2=4. But you don't have to go there with faith. Even though you really believe what you believe is true, you know it's hard to have faith and can imagine that someone else might not agree with you and actually not be an idiot. Faith kind of forces you to respect the other person more. Like with my friend who backs the other political candidate: I really do think she's wrong, and sometimes I can't believe she believes the things she says. But I know her. She's not an idiot. And she'd say the same about me. We just disagree. We have different beliefs.

Which brings us back to John. John knows there are all kinds of things we could believe about Jesus, but he wants us to believe that Jesus is the Messiah, God's Son. And he knows this isn't something you can prove, so instead he tries to persuade us by telling us a story big enough, true enough, that we might come to faith. He definitely believes it's true, and because of his writing and the rest of the Bible, so do I.

You know, I see that. I do. It's like John and other writers of the Bible are giving us a different kind of truth. Like you said before, it's *bigger* than facts.

That's a great way of putting it. In fact, it's why I think the Bible as a book of faith is worth reading.

What do you mean?

If the Bible's mainly a divine reference book, then the biblical writers are mostly sharing facts with us. But if they're confessing things they think are true but can't prove, then there's an urgency about it. They're not just worried about getting the facts right. Rather, they want to persuade us of this really huge, but at times hard to believe, truth that might just change our lives if we believe it.

When you look at it that way, it's like the Bible wants to go after the really big issues in life, the stuff that really matters.

Exactly. It's the difference between seeing the Bible as a divine reference book or as God's living, breathing, and active Word.

I like that: from divine reference book to living Word. Although phrasing it that way also brings up another big question.

No problem; I've definitely got the time. Let's keep talking.

Insights and Questions

CHAPTER 3

How Is the Bible the Word of God?

So, you said you had another big question.

Yeah, it seems like a lot of people call the Bible "the Word of God."

I think you're right. And I often do too.

To tell you the truth, I'm not totally sure what to make of that.

What do you mean?

Well, what does it mean to call the Bible the Word of God? Are we saying it's different from every other book? That it kind of fell from heaven or has special powers? That it's holy? I mean, we do call it "the Holy Bible," after all.

Yes, we do. Well, what do you think? How do you hear talk of the Bible being "Holy" and "the Word of God"?

I think it means it's special. You know, different. But I'm not sure how, exactly. A lot of the talk about the Bible I hear sounds like the "divine reference book" we were talking about earlier. I'm not sure how the Bible is the Word of God.

Let's try to get at it another way. We'll start with a little free association. You know, like I say "peanut butter" and you say . . .

Jelly.

That's right. Or if you're me, chocolate.

Chocolate?

Yeah, you know, like peanut butter cups. I love those things.

Okay, whatever, but could we . . .

Right, sorry—got a little distracted. Okay, so we'll do a little free association. When I say "Word of God," what comes to mind?

The Bible, of course—actually, a big, black, leather-bound Bible. And if I think about it, it's not hard to see a preacher striding the stage with the big, black Bible in one hand and pointing with the other hand. And when he talks about the Bible as the Word of God, he really means it. I mean, the way he says it, "Bible" suddenly has three syllables—you know, Bi-i-ble.

Wow. You've got quite the scene going. Great imagination.

Okay, so Word of God and Bible—we've got that. What else comes to mind?

Words like *truth, revelation, guidance, the Ten Commandments*. How's that?

Good. Very good. I think these are a lot of the kinds of things people think of when they hear the phrase "Word of God."

It's okay that I think of a variety of things?

Sure. Actually, some of this variety starts with the Bible itself, as it uses that phrase "Word of God" in a couple of different ways. And very early on the church took up that language too. Before long, there were at least three distinct and traditional ways Christians came to talk about "the Word of God." Over time, theologians called it—you guessed it—the "threefold understanding of the Word."

How original. Of the three, how many did I get?

One.

One? Hmmm. Not so great. I'm guessing that was "Bible."

Yup, it's the Bible. But don't feel bad—the other two aren't quite as obvious. Although I'm pretty sure you can get another. Think, for a second, about Jesus.

Jesus?

Yeah, Jesus as the Word of God.

Oh, sure. Like the reading from the beginning of John: "In the beginning was the Word."

Right. The very first verse of John's Gospel says, "In the beginning was the Word, and the Word was with God, and the Word was God." And then a little later, in verse 14, it says, "And the Word became flesh and lived among us."

The Word becoming flesh—that's Christmas, right?

Right. This is John's description of the incarnation, of God taking on our human flesh in Jesus, which we celebrate at Christmas. And John's way of describing all this is to call Jesus "the Word."

So that's two meanings. What's the other one?

This is the harder one, the one we don't think of that often. It's the gospel.

The gospel?

The gospel, the good news of what God has done for us and all the world in and through Jesus.

So it's Bible, Jesus, and the gospel?

Yes, although not necessarily in that order.

Jesus

WORD OF GOD

Gospel   Bible

What do you mean?

Well, the most powerful use of "Word of God" in the whole history of the church—the Bible and all the traditions that come after—is Jesus. John's use of that imagery in the poetic opening of his Gospel has captured the imagination of artists, hymn writers, theologians, and everyday church-goers for centuries.

Yes. "The Word made flesh." It's real. I can picture that.

The one most often quoted in the New Testament, though, is the "Word of God" as "gospel," the good news about Jesus. "Word of God" comes up in the letters of Paul all over the place as a kind of shorthand for "gospel." In fact, they're almost interchangeable. And the Gospel of Luke and its sequel, the Acts of the Apostles . . .

Sequel?

Luke and Acts together are something of a two-volume work. The Gospel of Luke is Part 1, telling us about Jesus, while Acts is Part 2, telling us about the beginning of the church.

Interesting . . .

In Acts especially, "Word of God" is used regularly to describe the preaching of the message about Jesus. Luke links the growth of the church to its proclamation of the Word; so that in Acts, the more the early church preaches the gospel, the more it grows.

Again, very interesting. But I have to say I'm a little surprised that the Bible isn't getting a little more attention here.

Just wait. The Bible doesn't actually call itself the Word of God.

Get out! Seriously?

Seriously. There is only one place that really even comes close. That's in 2 Timothy, where the author writes, "All scripture is inspired by God and is useful for teaching, for reproof, for correction, and for training in righteousness" (3:16).

So how come it seems as if the only way we think about the Word of God now is to think of the Bible?

Great question. On the one hand, the church has long claimed the Bible as the Word of God because, as we said before, the whole thing is a story about God, and Christians believe that the Bible is the best place for us to get to know God.

On the other hand, though, it's almost as if in recent years we think *only* about the Bible as being God's Word. We can forget that it's important not simply because of what it is, but because of what it *does*, which is testify to God and to God's work, especially in Jesus.

This is starting to get a little confusing.

Let me try to make it clearer by offering an analogy.

Okay.

I'll warn you from the get-go, though, that this is a long analogy.

Alright. Thanks. I've been warned.

What I want to do is to put to the side, for a minute, our discussion of the three-fold understanding of the Word.

That shouldn't be hard!

Smart aleck.

Alright, so we'll put it to the side for a bit, and instead I want to think about three different ways we experience life.

Life?

Yeah, life. The first way we experience life is at the level of what I call "event." The level at which stuff happens. All kinds of stuff happens all the time, of course, and each thing that happens occurs in a moment in time as a distinct event.

I'm with you so far. Stuff happens—sounds like a polite paraphrase of a bumper sticker popular not too long ago.

That's funny. I'd forgotten about that one.

Okay, so stuff happens—life as event. Now, the second way we experience life is at what I call the level of "meaning" or "significance." Think about it for a second. Of all the things that happen, only some of them are significant. That is, we attach meaning to a relatively small portion of all the stuff that happens to us. So when someone asks you what you did last weekend, you're likely as not to say . . .

"Nothing."

And is that true?

Well, no, not literally. I actually did lots of things.

So why do you say, "Nothing."

What I mean is, nothing that's really important, nothing worth talking about.

Nothing, you mean, with any particular meaning or significance.

I see. Okay, so the second way we experience life is at the level of significance. And the third way?

The third way we experience life is at what I call the level of "medium." That is, once something's happened that we decide is meaningful or significant, we need some way to pass it on, to share it with others.

That makes sense. After all, we're not telepathic. None of us can read minds, so we need some way to share the meaning of an event with each other.

That's right. Usually we use words, but sometimes it's music or painting or sculpture—there are all kinds of ways to share the significance of something we've experienced.

All right, let me see if I'm following. We experience life at three levels: event, significance, and medium.

Yes.

Event
===

EXPERIENCE LIFE

Significance   Medium

And the point of all this would be ... ?

> Fair enough. The point becomes clearer as we think about the relationship between these three.

Go on.

> We'll start with the first one, the level of event. Notice that it never lasts for long. In fact, the moment any event happens, the next moment it's gone.

Gone?

> Yeah. Simply because events happen in time. Once something—anything—has occurred, it's in the past and no longer available to us in the present. That's true of a brief conversation we had yesterday morning and of the two-hour soccer game we watched over the weekend. These things, all things, happen in time, and once they've happened, they're no longer available to us.

Except by memory.

> That's true. We bring past events into the present by memory, and so usually we don't worry about them being in the past. But sometimes we can't remember something, or don't trust our memories, or we might even disagree with others about what we remember. In each case, our link to this past event is weakened, or even evaporates.

No kidding. This seems to happen a lot with my kids, like when I've asked them to take out the garbage or set the table or get their homework done *before* texting a friend or finishing the book they're reading. When I ask them what

happened, it's as if I never told them. It feels to me as if they've just forgotten, because they weren't really paying attention to what I said in the first place.

We've all had moments like those. With the kids, with your spouse over who was supposed to order the pizza for supper, with a friend about which café you were meeting at for coffee. And each time you have different memories of the same event, you realize how cut off you are from it, because it lives in the past while you keep moving forward in time in the present.

I know. Sometimes I wish we could just videotape everything so I could run the tape backward and show my kids evidence of their promise to get their homework done first.

You really would want to videotape everything?

No, not really, that would be incredibly intrusive. But I do wish we had better access to the past. I guess that's why we rely so much on the media—to capture the past and keep it accessible to us.

Newspapers, books, video, and the rest are definitely a great source to connect with both current events and the past, but even these aren't totally reliable.

What do you mean?

Think how often the media gets something wrong, or when there are totally different reports. Compare Fox News and MSNBC the next time something big happens in Washington. It's like watching a broadcast about two different events.

Sure, but they're obviously biased; everyone knows that.

The same happens with newspapers and historians too. Different reporters or writers covering the same event will totally disagree on what happened. Sometimes the newspaper or author has just made a mistake and will retract it later, but other times there's no real agreement on what actually happened.

Maybe with politically charged events, but not when it comes to simple facts.

Okay, let's take the Million Man March in Washington, D.C., in the mid-1990s as an example.

Yeah, I remember that. But that wasn't exactly a politically neutral event. I mean, it was a protest on Washington led by some of the more controversial African American leaders in the country.

Fair enough. But it's also as good an example of covering the "facts" as I can think of. I mean, the argument was basically about how many people showed up.

Yeah. I think I remember. Didn't the organizers say that the number of people who showed up was three or four times more than the Park Service said? They even talked about going to court.

Right. Good memory. Various newspapers reported wildly different numbers, too, and a group of researchers examining photos of the event later offered different estimates still—and even those had a wide margin of error. Nobody could agree. After the controversy was over, in fact, Congress actually made a law prohibiting the Park Service from providing estimates of gatherings to avoid this kind of conflict in the future.

You'd think if there was anything you could get right, it'd be counting people.

Precisely. And video is no better. Think of the Rodney King beating in L.A. that was caught on video, and still people couldn't agree on what actually happened. Even with YouTube and all the other video outlets that exist today, we still live with a gap, a time gap, between the present and past events, even recently past events, let alone distant ones.

I can see that. But how does that relate to what we're talking about?

It means that, as much as we might like to, we can never remain at the level of event. We know this level exists—it's where we experience things—but we can't stay there when it comes to individual events. The past is past, and we live in the present. So we're always pushed to move to the level of significance.

The level at which we attach meaning?

Right. We generally remember a particular event—whether it was something that happened or something someone said—precisely because we've attached some significance to it. What we hold on to isn't as much the actual event as what it means to us.

That makes sense.

The tricky thing, though, is that this level is always a matter of interpretation, of confession.

Confession? Why confession?

Think of it this way. Whatever significance or meaning we attach to a past event is something we *assign* to it. Meaning isn't obvious; it's not inherent in the past event itself. It's something we read into it. And it's not something we can prove. We can give good reasons why we might believe something, but in the end we can only confess it; we can't prove it.

That reminds me of an argument I once had with a college classmate about who the greatest president was. I said it was Lincoln, and she didn't buy it. We must've argued for an hour, but everything I said she countered. Like when I said the Emancipation Proclamation showed Lincoln's commitment to freedom, she said that it was politically motivated. In the end, there was just no way we could settle it.

Who did she think the greatest president was?

Washington, Jefferson, Madison, Monroe. She'd take any of these over Lincoln. Of course, her home was in . . .

Let me guess—could it be the great Commonwealth of Virginia?

You got it!

Well, perspective matters. Where we're standing shapes how we see things, even what we see in the first place. We'd like to think it doesn't, but it just does.

Speaking of Lincoln, do you remember the controversy when Ken Burns made his documentary on the Civil War?

Yeah. I think folks from the South wondered why this guy from New Hampshire was making the definitive record of the War and didn't trust that their perspective would be treated with equal respect.

We can't even agree on what to call it. Some call it the Civil War, while others the War between the States. You'd think regional differences wouldn't shape our viewpoint on history so much.

Oh, I don't know. I think that's not all that uncommon. In fact, there's actually something similar going on in the Bible.

Really?

Yup. There are actually two versions of the history of Israel, one recorded in the books of 1 and 2 Samuel and 1 and 2 Kings and another in the books of 1 and 2 Chronicles.

That sounds like six books, not two.

In biblical times, when a book got to a certain length, they just stopped and started another one. It usually had to do with scroll length. So there's essentially the Chronicles tradition and the Kings tradition, which includes both 1 and 2 Samuel and 1 and 2 Kings.

Why did they need two accounts?

It's not unlike the Civil War question. Israel was made up of 12 tribes that belonged to two distinct coalitions. These were brought together and united under King David but split apart later. Interestingly, as in the United States, there was a southern alliance and a northern alliance, and each had its own version of Israel's history. Though they were similar in many details, their historical traditions often differed at important points.

Like?

Like with David, for instance. David was from the tribe of Judah, one of the southern tribes.

So David was a southern boy?

You might say that.

So not surprisingly, the Chronicles account, which was written from the southern perspective, was a little more generous to David than the other version.

In what way?

Well, for starters, Chronicles doesn't make any mention of Bathsheba.

You're kidding! Everyone knows about David and Bathsheba!

You're right; it is a very well-known story. And it comes from 2 Samuel, part of the Kings tradition. This tradition was written by folks sympathetic to the northern tribes, and they were never as crazy about David as the southern tribes were, so they spared no details about his failings.

I guess if I ever have a biography written about me, I'll want to make sure it's from someone who really likes me.

Good idea.

Well, this all helps me appreciate your point that we can't prove the meaning or significance of events.

That's what I mean by confession. History is ambiguous. We have to assign it meaning, and the meaning we assign is our interpretation, our confession.

I think I've got it. Lots of things happen—that's the level of *event*. Some really matter to us—that's the level of *significance*. But the significance or meaning we attach to something that has happened isn't something we can prove; it's a matter of interpretation.

Very good. And that brings us to the third level.

Go on.

When we talked about the level of event, we said we *can't* stay there, because time keeps moving on. With the level of meaning, though, it's more like we *don't want* to stay there.

Don't want to?

No, not really. While it might be possible to keep a sense of the meaning of some event to ourselves, usually we don't want to because we want to communicate it. And if we want to share the meaning and significance of something, then we need some kind of medium, or record, some vehicle we can use to communicate what we think is significant about something that happened.

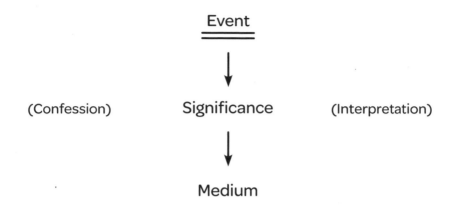

So this is the level that really matters, then?

It certainly does matter, because if we want to share what we're thinking, we need some medium. I mean, none of us is telepathic. We can't just send our thoughts to each other through some kind of mind meld. We need some way, some medium—words, signs, something—to communicate.

But as important as medium is, we can't stay at this level either.

Why not?

The medium isn't set up for that.

Sorry, you've lost me.

Let me try again. A medium—whether it's words on a page, notes on a score, or paint on a canvas—is a means of communication. Its whole purpose is to direct our attention to something else, to whatever it was intended to communicate.

For instance, while you may admire the kind of paper a book is printed with, or the font the publishing house chose, that's hardly your focus when you pick up a book. What you're interested in is the message or story the font, paper, binding, and the rest communicate.

The same is true of a writer's style. So while we may pay a lot of attention to the particular style or rhetorical conventions of a writer—Emily Dickinson's use of the dash, or Hemingway's mini-malist prose, or Tom Wolfe's attention to popular culture—we notice these things not because we're interested primarily in the use of punc-tuation, spare prose, or pop culture, but because it's through these things that the authors convey to us the meaning they want to share.

That makes sense, but now I'm not so sure how important the medium really is. I mean, if it's just a container, why are we giving it much attention at all?

Great question.

On the one hand, the medium is very important, because it's where we find the meaning another is trying to communicate. That is, if I want to experience what Laura Ingalls Wilder is trying to share in *Little House on the Prairie*, then there's no substitute for reading the book. What she wants to share is all there. Her book holds that meaning, and it's the way she gives me access to it, the way she shares that meaning.

But it's not the only way.

What do you mean?

You can talk with someone else who read the book.

True, although that won't be quite the same. I'll have the meaning second-hand, through the lens of the person who read it.

You could also watch the television show based on the book.

Great point. That would be a very immediate experience of meaning, but again, it would be through the lens of someone else—in this case, the script writer, director, and actors. You'd certainly get something of what Laura Ingalls Wilder wanted to share, assuming the show is faithful to the book, but you'd also get the interpretations and values of the people who made the book into a television program.

Which is, of course, another reason why medium is so important.

How so?

Because you can't finally separate meaning from its medium. When we choose a particular medium, the meaning we want to share gets bound up in that medium. Which is why the book and the T.V. program are very similar, but not the same.

I have that experience all the time with movies made from my favorite books. Whether it's *Harry Potter* or *The Hunt for Red October*, the movie is never quite the same.

Right. And while usually we complain the movie isn't as good as the book, what we're really noticing is that it's just different, sometimes a little, sometimes a lot, but there is something different being shared. The film becomes as much a medium for the script writer, director, and actors as it is for the original author.

So even though meaning and medium are distinct, you can't really separate them.

That reminds me of watching an interview of an author who'd written a book we were discussing in my book club. The interviewer asked if the author could sum up her book in a few sentences. She really tried, but it was hard. I suppose if she could really just tell us in a minute what her book meant, she probably wouldn't have spent all those years writing it. I mean, we talked about it for two hours and weren't nearly done. To get that level of meaning, someone else's summary wouldn't do, not even the author's. You just had to read the book.

I think that's just it. You can talk about the meaning of something, but the medium doesn't just hold that meaning, like a jar holding honey. The medium actually shapes that meaning and can't be totally separated from it. You can talk about a book's meaning, but it took that book to bring that meaning to expression, at least to expression in that particular way. So the book is incredibly important.

And yet the whole reason she wrote that book was to share something she felt was profoundly true and important.

Exactly. Which means the medium is incredibly important but finally exists always to point beyond itself to the meaning it is communicating.

Okay, I think I've almost got it. Lots of things—events—happen. Most we don't pay attention to, but some we believe are significant or meaningful. We

can't really prove what something means once and for all, but we can share what we *believe* it means. To do that we need a medium that holds and shapes that meaning. The medium doesn't just exist for itself, but it exists to point us to that meaning.

Very well put.

Thanks. Though I have to admit I'm still figuring this out.

Understandable. Even though this is the way we experience and make sense of life all the time, we never sit back to think about it.

So let me try an example from my own life to pull it together.

That might be helpful.

Nine months after we were married, my wife Karin was struck by a car while walking across the street in front of our apartment to get some groceries from the car.

Oh my goodness! Was she alright?

She was, thanks. She had a minor concussion and was released from the hospital the same day.

The next day, we went down to the town hall to file our report on what happened for insurance purposes. When we got there, there were already three other eyewitness reports, making four in all—let's call them Matthew, Mark, Luke, and John . . .

Very funny.

Just kidding.

In addition to my wife's, there was a report offered by the driver and another from someone sitting in a parked car. In fact, it was this person my wife turned to greet as she was crossing the street and so didn't see the oncoming car. The fourth report was from the driver of a car about a hundred yards behind the car that hit my wife.

You didn't see it?

No, I was inside and only came out after a neighbor shouted for me right after Karin was hit.

Okay, so four eyewitness reports. That should've made the insurance company happy, plenty of evidence of what happened.

Yeah, except they didn't agree.

You're kidding!

No. They divided essentially into two camps. One—made up of my wife and the person in the parked car—essentially told the same story I told you: Karin was crossing the street, turned to greet our neighbor in the parked car, didn't see the oncoming car, and was side-swiped. The other, offered by the driver who hit her and the driver a hundred yards back, said that Karin was about to cross the street when she leaped out into the middle of the street into the way of the car that hit her.

Uh oh! How did your wife feel about that?

She was really, really mad. But of course we had no way to prove it. They were all eyewitnesses, and there was no going back to that moment in time the day before.

Why do you think they did that? And did it cause any problems?

The insurance company was great, so there were no problems. And I don't think the two people did it on purpose or for any bad reasons.

Then why? I mean, how could they see something totally different from what your wife saw?

Well, I remember that when the accident happened, all kinds of people gathered to see what was going on and to offer support. One group was gathered around Karin and me, and included our neighbor. Another was gathered around the driver who hit Karin, because she, the driver, was also understandably very upset. The driver of the other car was in that group too.

The two groups were really close together, and I remember overhearing what the folks in the other group were saying as they tried to comfort the driver. Things like, "I'm sure she'll be okay." "I'm sure everything will work out." "She probably just jumped in front of you."

So you think that they were saying things that were comforting, and that made a certain kind of sense, and that that's what they came to believe?

Sure. I mean, it's not like our memory is the best when we're upset, and I think we often put things together—things we saw, things we thought we saw, things people say we saw, things we wanted to see. It's not about being truthful or untruthful at this point; it's just the way memory works to help us deal with the present.

In any event, no matter how embarrassed my wife might be that there's a public record that she once jumped into the path of oncoming traffic, there's just no getting back to that moment to prove things differently. That event happened in the past, but we're in the present, and there's no crossing the time gap to get back to it.

Yeah, I definitely can see that.

Now, at the level of significance it gets even more interesting.

I'm pretty sure that of all the people that were there—neighbors, bystanders, ambulance folks, and so forth—probably only three of us really remember it at all. The other driver, of course, probably rarely thinks of it, and when she does she is probably just relieved nothing bad came of it.

I'm guessing your wife is another who remembers.

Absolutely. And I think the significance of this event for her came out a few years later when our firstborn, who was around four at the time, was struggling to pull his hand free from hers when we were crossing the street so he could run on ahead. Karin wouldn't let his hand go, and when he asked, "Mommy, when will I be old enough to cross the street without holding your hand?" Karin answered immediately, without even thinking, "When you're 26!"

Twenty-six?!

Well, she was 25 when she got hit, and I think she figured that, clearly, that was not old enough!

Very funny.

We did eventually let him cross the road without holding our hands, but for Karin that accident really made her aware of the need to be careful around streets.

So the third person—and probably the only other person—who thinks about this day is me. And I attach a very different kind of significance to it, because that's the day I realized just how fragile life is. I mean, it wasn't just my wife lying on the road, it was my whole life suddenly at risk.

I've had this feeling each of the times one of my kids was born, too—that life is fragile, vulnerable, that whenever you're really attached to someone—a spouse, child, parent, sibling—you become captive to fate, hostage to destiny. You realize that so many things beyond your control can happen to your loved one.

That sense of things can make life scary.

And precious too. But that's what has stayed with me.

And to share this meaning with you just now, I've told you a story. If I were more talented, I might've written a poem called "Ode to Karin's Accident," or something, or composed a sonata, maybe called . . .

Opus #1, I'm guessing, since you don't write music!

No kidding. I have next to no musical ability, so I'm stuck with words.

Although words seem usually to get the job done pretty well!

Yes, they do. And the words I've chosen, and the way I've told it, both hold and shape the meaning I want to share. And if you want to share in it, you've got to pay attention to those words. But finally the words themselves point to something else, to something bigger, to the meaning about how fragile and precious life is that I want to share.

That makes sense.

Let me see if I have this, then. We experience life at the level of event. We attach meaning or significance to some of those events, and that meaning is always a matter of interpretation, of confession. We use different media to share that meaning. And while the medium is very important, it points us back to that meaning.

Exactly right.

I think that makes the level of meaning or significance the most important one.

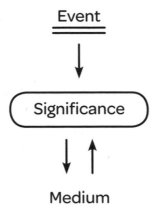

I think you're right. All the levels are important, but the one that matters to us most is the level of meaning. That's where, if you will, we really live, where we have the most at stake.

We get at this with the distinction between two very similar words in English, *historical* and *historic*. *Historical* describes anything that happened in time, in history, whereas *historic* describes something that happened in the past and still makes a difference to us in the present. So while every political speech we may hear is historical, a few—such as Lincoln's Second Inaugural Address and the Gettysburg Address—are historic.

Okay, I think I've got it. And I think I'm able to guess, at this point, what all this might have to do with the Bible as the Word of God.

Yes?

Well, I'm guessing Jesus, the actual man who lived back then, is at the level of event.

That's right.

And we definitely can't get back to him. Although it seems as if a lot of people try. I mean, I've seen some of the different biographies of Jesus.

I've seen those too. And the interesting thing is that while they agree on a few points, they disagree on a lot more. Which is probably good if they want to sell more books!

No kidding.

About 100 years ago, Albert Schweitzer wrote a book about the "quest" for the historical Jesus.

Albert Schweitzer, the doctor who went to Africa?

Yeah, he was also a biblical scholar.

Really?

And an organist and Bach scholar.

Talented guy!

Very.

Anyway, he wrote this book and near the end concluded, as he put it, that whenever you peer down into the deep well of history trying to glimpse Jesus, you are as likely to see your own reflection as Jesus' reflection.

Why did he say that?

Because our judgments about the past are always an interpretation, a confession, that is shaped by who we are and what we believe.

In fact, whenever I open up a book on the historical Jesus, I first read the biographical information about the author to give me a clue about what conclusions the author might come to.

So if Jesus is the level of event, then the gospel, the message about Jesus, is the level of meaning and significance?

Right again. This gospel is essentially a confession of faith. The people who wrote about Jesus wanted to report not only what Jesus did, but also what it meant to them and what it still might mean for us today. Not everyone agreed with the early Christians. Some people thought Jesus was crazy; others thought he was a criminal. But some thought he was the Son of God and that through him God was acting to save the world. This was the confession of the people who wrote the New Testament, what we call the "gospel."

That means the Bible is the medium.

Yup.

Which means that the Bible is incredibly important because it is the place you find the gospel, but its job is to point beyond itself to that gospel.

Exactly. This is what I'd call a "functional" understanding of biblical authority.

Functional?

"Functional" in the sense that we value the Bible not because of what it *is*—somehow different in its very nature or essence from everything else—but because of what it *does*: point to the gospel. And that function, to point to the gospel, is what makes it different, special, and authoritative for Christians.

And we call it "the Word of God" because of what it does, pointing to the gospel.

Right. We confess that God spoke and still speaks through the gospel the Bible holds.

Martin Luther had a nice way of capturing this when he described the Bible as the manger that holds the Christ child. To follow his analogy, if you're one of the magi looking for the Christ child, there's only way place to look, and it's not in Jerusalem or Rome but in Bethlehem, and once you're in Bethlehem, you can't go to the best hotel but to the stable behind an inn where the babe is resting in a manger. But, Luther goes on to say, once you've found the manger, be careful lest you fall down on your knees to worship the wood and straw of the manger instead of the baby.

So we're called to value the Bible very highly because it holds the gospel, but to be careful that we don't worship the Bible for its own sake. It's important because of what it holds, the gospel.

Yes. Although here again it's helpful to remember what we said about all mediums. They don't just hold things, like some kind of suitcase or jar. They actually participate in the meaning they hold, and they make it possible to share that meaning with future generations. Which makes the Bible incredibly important for Christians.

So the Bible doesn't exist for its own sake, but for the gospel, precisely to share the gospel?

Right. And the Bible itself gives clues to that. We've already looked at one passage like that.

We have?

Yes, it's near the end of John's Gospel, where John, as you said, comes clean on what he's up to.

I remember. He said something like: Jesus did many other signs that the disciples saw, but those weren't written in this book—John's Gospel. But the ones that did get into the book were written for a reason—so that people would believe that Jesus is the Messiah, the Son of God, and that through believing they may have life in his name.

Good memory.

And I remember we said it was near the end of the Gospel, right?

Yes. John 20:30-31.

So all the writing John does, all the choices he makes, are toward offering us a medium—his gospel—to point us to the larger meaning or significance of Jesus—the confession that Jesus is God's Son, and that if we believe this we'll have life. This isn't something that John can prove, but it is something that, while it happened long ago, still makes a difference to women and men today.

Which means that of the three ways to understand "Word of God" we talked about, it's the middle one, the gospel, that is the most important.

Maybe a better word than *important* would be to say it's the most immediate, or most relevant, in that it communicates why the story of Jesus still matters to us today.

Like *historical* and *historic*?

Exactly. If the apostle Paul had only said, "Jesus died," he would have been talking about a historical event, but he goes on to interpret that event, saying, "Jesus died for our sins." That is a confession of faith about something that is historic, because it happened in the past but it still makes a difference to us today.

It sounds like the gospel—the level of significance and meaning—is really where the action is. I mean, we can't get back to Jesus as past event, although that's obviously where it all started, where God got involved. And we love our Bible as a great medium, but even the Bible points us beyond itself back to the gospel.

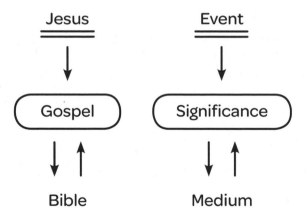

That's right. The reformers—Martin Luther and his colleagues—used to talk about the gospel as God's "living voice."

Because what the Bible says still makes a difference to us today. Yeah, that makes sense.

So, three ways to understand "the Word of God":
Jesus **is God in human form, the Word of God made flesh.**

The *gospel* **is the confession of faith of what God did through Jesus and why that matters to us today, and so is the living Word of God.**

And the *Bible* **tells the story of God's love for the world throughout history, and that story culminates in the gospel, the story of Jesus, and so is God's written Word.**

Very nicely put.

Does that make sense?

It does. A lot of sense, actually. Although . . .

Let me guess: you've got another question.

Of course.

Great. Let's take a little break and then get to it.

Insights and Questions

CHAPTER 4

Where Did the Bible Come From?

I want to talk a little more about the Bible.

Sure. I've enjoyed the conversation so far.

Well, we said that we value the Bible because of what it *does*—I think you said this was its function, right?

Right.

So we value what it *does* more than what it *is*.

Yes.

So what exactly is it? I mean, how do we describe what it is? I know we said it was like a collection of books. And we said that the Bible is like the manger holding the Christ child—something that's more or less ordinary in and of itself but that's extraordinary because of what it holds and does.

Yup.

Does that mean, then, that the Bible is a completely human book, like all other books?

In one way, yes, that's what it means.

In one way?

Yes. It is a book written by humans, and so in this respect it's like all other books. At the same time, it is also God's book. Through it God achieves God's divine purposes, so it is also different from all other books.

"God's divine purposes"?

The Bible tells us the story of God's relationship with humanity. By reading it and being drawn into that story we come to know and believe just how much God loves us. So, we desire to be in relationship with God. And drawing us into a relationship of love is exactly what God wants, what God *purposes* or intends through Scripture.

Such as the part where John writes, "But these are written so that you will come to believe . . ." and so on.

Yes, that's what's going on. John writes his Gospel so that we might believe Jesus is God's Son and know how much God loves us in and through Jesus. John wants his readers—including us—to be drawn into relationship with God. When this happens we have, as John writes, life.

So the Bible is human in terms of its nature, but divine in terms of its function?

I think that captures things pretty well.

This isn't all that different, when I think about it, from our earlier conversation about King David, Peter, and all the other ordinary, and even complicated, people in the Bible that God uses to get God's work done.

That's true. God regularly takes ordinary people and does extraordinary things through them. I think that's happening with the Bible too. It's something that is essentially ordinary, and yet God uses it to accomplish something extraordinary.

That sounds very different from the divine reference book we were talking about earlier. I mean, sometimes when folks who treat the Bible as a reference book talk about it, it sounds like the Bible sort of fell from heaven.

Well, there are religions that believe their scriptures are "ontologically" different; that is, different in their very nature or being. And some religions do, in fact, think their sacred writings literally fell from heaven or were delivered to mortals by divine beings. But by and large, Christians haven't thought that way.

But what about all this talk about "inspiration" and "inerrancy" you hear from some Christians? That sounds pretty otherworldly, or at least a lot more divine than human.

Let's take each of those terms in turn.

Okay.

"Inspiration" is used one time in the Bible itself, in 2 Timothy 3:16. We looked at that verse early on in our discussion about the Bible as the Word of God.

I remember: "All Scripture is inspired by God and is useful for teaching, for reproof, for correction, and for training in righteousness."

Right. And I think that most, if not all, Christians believe the Bible is inspired by God. After all, we've said that the Bible is a collection of confessions, and the people who made those confessions were, quite literally, so inspired by their experience of God, so filled by God's Spirit, that they just couldn't keep it to themselves—they had to confess. Moreover, the story the Bible tells through these confessions of faith is, as we've seen, all about God and God's relationship with us. So I definitely think the Bible is inspired by God, and I think it's useful for teaching, correcting, and training, as the letter to Timothy says.

When you put it that way, I do too. But I don't think that's what people mean when they talk about the Bible being inspired. It sounds more like they think God gave the writers the exact words to use, kind of like they were taking dictation.

That's where the second term comes in—"inerrant."

Go on.

Well, *inerrant* is not a term used in the Bible. And it only became popular in the church within the last century or so, which isn't so long when you think that Jesus and the disciples lived 2,000 years ago and the events of the Old Testament are more like 3,000 and 4,000 years ago.

Essentially, *inerrancy* means that there are no factual errors. Everything the Bible says about faith, about life, about history, geography, and science is factually accurate.

There's a softer version, called "infallibility," that says there may be mistakes in minor details, but that there are no mistakes when it comes to major issues like faith and doctrine. But it really amounts to pretty much the same thing. The Bible is divine, authored by God, without error, and so forth, at least in the original manuscripts.

The original manuscripts?

For more than 1,000 years—up until the 16th century and the invention of the printing press—the Bible was copied by hand. There are literally thousands of these copies around, most dating from the Middle Ages. The earliest complete copies of some books of the Bible we have are from the fourth century, a couple of centuries after the books of the New Testament were written. We also have some fragments that were written earlier, some as early as the second century, but these are mostly just little pieces of one book or another.

There are loads of differences between these various manuscripts and fragments—mistakes in copying, slight differences of word choice or translation here and there, pieces missing from one version or another. Stuff like that.

So what we're reading today isn't the original.

The Bible we read is based on the oldest and most reliable manuscripts and was compiled from a close comparison of everything that was available. Scholars, from the most conservative to the most liberal, agree that it's probably about as close to the original books as possible.

Okay, so there are no original copies available. But some Christians still believe the Bible we have is not just inspired, but inerrant. So they really do think God just dictated the Bible to various writers?

The theory is that God used the distinct personalities and styles of the original writers but guided them to write something without error. So, not quite divine dictation, but pretty close.

Still seems like the Bible is essentially divine.

I guess I just don't see why this makes such a difference. I mean, when people talk about this they get really worked up.

Well, think about it a little. Given what we've talked about so far, why would this be really important for some people to believe?

I'll give you a hint: the answer has nothing to do with gymnastics.

What? Oh—the fact-value split! I get it. If you believe that something is true only if it's factually accurate, then you need to make sure every fact checks out.

Right. Hence the 500 and 600-page books "resolving" discrepancies and inconsistencies in the biblical witness.

And this is where the difference between that view and what we've been working at comes into play. I just don't think the biblical writers thought about truth this way. Truth was so much bigger than facts.

So, like we talked about before, many of the things that are most important to us—that we believe most strongly are true—can't be reduced to facts you can prove or disprove.

And, even notions of historical accuracy are very much a product of post-Enlightenment Europe. In pre-modern times, historical narrative was intended to educate, to enrich, and to ennoble, not primarily to capture some supposedly neutral record of events. That doesn't mean histories written during that time had no relation to actual events, like some kind of fiction. But it does mean that when you wrote a history you were trying to get the *truth* of what happened across—that is, its meaning and significance. So when we imagine the biblical writers having the same concerns as a 21st-century journalist, we're not only imposing our categories on their writing but we also risk missing the point of what they are trying to achieve in the first place.

Frankly, I'm not sure that much has really changed today. I mean, I know we're concerned about facts and all, but think about some of the fights we have over what goes into history textbooks and state-wide history tests. People have a lot invested in making sure the history our kids learn is the history we want taught.

Great point. Yet we still tend to think of history as a neutral account of the past, and we still tend to think that if something isn't factually accurate, it's not true. For good or ill, that's part of our inheritance from the Enlightenment.

And if you operate with this point of view in terms of the Bible, then making sure that all the facts add up becomes incredibly important.

Okay, so that helps me understand why some Christians stress the Bible's divine nature so much. But why do you stress its humanity so much?

Actually, I want to keep a balance. I want to say that the Bible is both ordinary and extraordinary, both human and divine, not simply one or the other.

Fifty-fifty—half human and half divine?

Not exactly. I'd say more like 100 percent human and 100 percent divine.

Which leaves you with 200 percent. That doesn't exactly add up.

Not if you think about it as a math problem. But I want to go back to what we said earlier. The Bible is totally human, totally ordinary, in terms of what it *is*—a collection of confessions made by very human people so gripped by their experience of God they had to give witness to that experience. At the same time, the Bible is totally divine in terms of what it *does* or, maybe better, in terms of how God uses it to accomplish something extraordinary. I believe God uses these human confessions of faith to speak to people today, to bring them to faith and into relationship with God, achieving God's divine purpose.

So, totally human and totally divine.

That sounds a lot like some words in one of the creeds we say in church.

You're probably thinking about the Nicene Creed, which was written in the fourth century. It's something of a consensus statement regarding some big questions the early church had about whether Jesus was human or divine. They ended up saying he was both, describing him as "fully God and fully man."

That's the part I was thinking of. It sounds a lot like what you just said about the Bible.

You're right, it does sound similar. It's important to note that the early church wasn't just saying that Jesus was human and God *used* him to do something divine. The early church was saying that Jesus actually *was* God and at the same time *was* human, that he had two natures at once.

And is that what you're saying about the Bible?

I don't think we need to make that claim for the Bible. Certainly the Bible doesn't, and neither did early Christians.

At the same time, though, I think there is something similar going on with our discussion about Scripture, at least in terms of the belief that God uses things that are really human to achieve God's work. God doesn't need to change something, or make it no longer human, or require it to be perfect, before God will use it.

Ultimately, the question isn't whether the Bible has two natures, like Jesus. Rather, the question is whether the Bible, as a product of human beings' experiences and reflections, can participate in the divine, can be used by God to achieve God's divine purpose of bringing people into relationship with God.

And that's so important because . . . ?

Well, think about it. Why do you think it's important that God uses the ordinary to accomplish extraordinary things? You've already given an answer to this question.

Okay, I get it. Because that's the way God always seems to work, like with King David and Peter.

Exactly. And David and Peter aren't the exceptions. All through the Bible, God again and again takes ordinary people—Abraham and Sarah, Moses and Miriam, the judges and prophets, the disciples and evangelists—to accomplish the things God wants to get done. All these people were ordinary men and women, just like you and me! Yet God used them to do God's work.

I know we've talked about this before, but I have to say that it still feels a little weird to think of the people in the Bible as being like us. You grow up kind of thinking that they're holier, more saintly.

Maybe at first, but not once you get reading. My goodness, you see they've got the same questions, the same problems, the same insecurities and dysfunctions as we do. Read very far and you're soon amazed that God would choose such ordinary, complicated, even problematic people to do God's work, but that's exactly the way the Bible tells it.

Which I guess is good news if we're supposed to imagine that God can also use us.

Exactly. Remember, again, that according to the Bible God isn't finished yet, and we live somewhere between the Acts of the Apostles and Revelation. So now it's our turn to take part in the ongoing story of how God intends to love, bless, and save this world.

That's why it matters that the Bible's a very ordinary, very human book—because, according to the Bible itself, God regularly uses ordinary, everyday, human means to accomplish God's extraordinary and divine purposes.

That makes sense, but if it really is a human book, then that raises a few questions of its own.

More than I few questions, I'd say.

Where do you want to start?

Well, let's start with who wrote the Bible.

Lots of people.

Hmm. I was looking for something a little more specific.

I'm sure, but unfortunately it's hard to be more specific. Think again about the Bible as a library, a collection of books. In all those books are a collection of confessions. There are just lots of people who were involved in writing down these confessions, collecting them, editing them, and sharing them with future generations.

Okay, let's slow down. I can understand that different people wrote different parts. But what's this about collecting and editing them? That isn't exactly the picture I had from Sunday school.

I know what you mean.

Let me try to explain by looking to a New Testament passage for an example.

That might be helpful. Where are we going to look?

We've already looked at the verses at the end of John's Gospel, in which he talks about some of the choices he made about which stories of Jesus to share.

Yeah, I remember: "Now Jesus did many other signs in the presence of his disciples, which are not written in this book. But these are written . . ." It's tempting to wonder about the "other signs" John talks about, but I suppose he had his reasons for picking the ones he did.

Yes, John is very clear that there were other stories of Jesus around, and he carefully chose the particular stories he shares in order to tell us the meaning and significance of Jesus in the hope that we will believe.

But that's not the only place a biblical writer "comes clean" about what he's up to. Luke does the same thing. But while John lets us in on what he's doing near the end of his Gospel, Luke gives us a picture of what he's up to right at the beginning of his. So we'll turn there now and see something similar going on.

> *Since many have undertaken to set down an orderly account of the events that have been fulfilled among us, just as they were handed on to us by those who from the beginning were eyewitnesses and servants of the word, I too decided, after investigating everything carefully from the very first, to write an orderly account for you, most excellent Theophilus, so that you may know the truth concerning the things about which you have been instructed.* (Luke 1:1-4)

It's an interesting opening, but why are we looking here?

Just as with other stories, the way a Gospel starts gives certain clues to what's coming. So it's helpful to give attention to the opening. For instance, Matthew is very interested in his readers seeing Jesus as the fulfillment of the Old Testament promises about the Messiah, so he starts with a genealogy that traces Jesus' ancestry to King David and through David back to Abraham.

Mark, on the other hand, starts with only a single sentence—which previews Mark's terse, fast-paced style—that reveals Jesus' identity as the Son of God to his readers. This is interesting, too, because it's not till near the end of the actual narrative, at the cross, that Jesus' divine identity is affirmed, and by someone you'd never suspect.

In John's case, because he wants to link what God is doing in Jesus, the world-redeeming Word made flesh, to God's world-creating Word at creation, he starts his Gospel with his poetic hymn to the Word that starts out, significantly, "In the beginning . . ."

And Luke?

Luke is actually the only evangelist who writes what we'd call a proper literary introduction, similar to what other writers of his time used. He starts by offering a brief statement of the purpose of his Gospel and by dedicating his work to a patron, in this case Theophilus.

So who's Theophilus?

We don't actually know. The name, in Greek, means "lover of God." It could be a person who encouraged Luke and even supported him monetarily so he could write his Gospel. Or Luke may use the name to suggest a whole community for whom he writes. Figuring out who Theophilus is may be beyond us; what's both more immediate and more interesting is what Luke tells Theophilus.

Like . . .

Well, what do you make of Luke saying he's putting together an account of the things that happened, "just as they were handed on to us by those who from the beginning were eyewitnesses?"

It sounds as if Luke wasn't actually there. That Luke *wasn't* an eyewitness, but is relying on what other people told him.

Yes, from this passage we can say with some certainly that Luke wasn't a witness to the events he describes, that he's probably a second- or even third-generation Christian.

I have to say that this isn't the way I'd always imagined it. I mean, I grew up more or less assuming that the Gospel writers were right there on the scene, kinda like the "Eyewitness News Team" on T.V. You know, "This is Luke. I'm standing outside the manger as shepherds begin to gather. Film at eleven."

That's what most of us grew up believing.

But here it's clear that not only was Luke not there, but that he's not the only one collecting stories about Jesus. After all, he says, "Since *many* have undertaken to set down an orderly account of the events . . ."

Well, we know of at least three others, whether or not Luke knew them all.

What? Oh, right: Matthew, Mark, and John.

And there were more still. In recent years, all kinds of collections of stories about Jesus from the early centuries have been discovered. Some are in the form of larger narratives, while others just seem to be smaller collections of his teachings, sayings, or miracles. You've probably heard of some of these—the Gospel of Thomas, the Gospel of Judas. They've gotten a lot of attention recently.

Yeah, I have heard of them. And Luke knew about all of these?

Probably not, as most of these were most likely written well after Luke. But he clearly knows of some other collections, as he mentions them here at the opening of his own Gospel.

And it sounds as if Luke is sorting through them all so that he can provide Theophilus with what he calls "an orderly account."
You know, it's interesting: he doesn't say the "right account" or the "true account" or the "only account," but an "orderly account." What does he mean by that?

That's a great question. Let me try to explain by way of an analogy.

You seem to like to explain things that way.

Call me simple, but stories really help me think things through.

Me too, actually. Go ahead.

Okay, so almost 20 years ago, I was traveling from San Diego to Seattle with a friend. We had planned our trip carefully, driving up the California coast to Sequoia National Park to see the giant redwoods, then going to Yosemite, then on to San Francisco to visit a friend and see the sights, and finally up through Portland to Seattle.

Sounds like a great trip.

It was . . . almost. Everything went as planned on the first leg of the trip, but as we were coming toward Yosemite from Sequoia, white smoke started billowing out from under the hood of my car.

Uh oh.

No kidding. Several gaskets had blown. It was a major repair.

What did you do?

Fortunately, I had AAA Plus, so I had the car towed to Fresno, which was about halfway to San Francisco. I called my San Francisco friend, who came and picked us up. We toured the city for three or four days while the car was worked on. When it was ready, my friend drove us back to Fresno, we picked up the car, and continued on to Yosemite. After camping there for a couple of days, we went back to San Francisco and stayed with our friend a few more days to see some of things we'd missed the first time. Then we continued with the rest of the trip as planned.

Great story, and the point would be . . .?

Well, when I got my pictures from the trip and put them in an album, I put them together in the order of the way things were *supposed* to have happened: Sequoia, Yosemite, San Francisco, Seattle.

What, no pictures of Fresno?

Well, the garage mechanics and other people we met there were great, but it didn't occur to me to take pictures, and it wasn't really the part of the trip I wanted to remember.

You see, I wasn't trying to produce an unbiased account of what happened; I was trying to tell a story that made sense, a story that shared my experiences out West, a story that would convey the truth of what I learned, felt, saw, and experienced. So I didn't split my San Francisco pictures. I put them together, because what mattered wasn't that they were separated by a few days in Yosemite, but the impression of San Francisco I was trying to capture and share.

And you think that's what Luke's doing? What he means by "an orderly account"?

Something like that. He says right up front that there are other orderly accounts out there. He doesn't argue about them or dispute them; he just says he's going to write his own orderly account so that Theophilus can be confident of the things he's already learned about the Christian faith.

So he's writing with Theophilus in mind, whether that's one person or a whole community?

I think so. He seems to know Theophilus and be familiar with what Theophilus has been taught. More than that, he wants to confirm Theophilus in his faith, maybe addressing some questions or clearing up certain issues through the way he tells his Gospel.

It seems as if he's telling a particular version of the story to make sense of things for the people he's writing for. So it's not as if there was something wrong with the other versions—as if he didn't like Matthew or Mark—but that they just weren't written for the folks he had in mind, the folks who maybe had asked him to write his Gospel in the first place.

Exactly. The different early Christian communities very likely had different questions, depending on all kinds of factors, such as whether they were primarily Jewish or Gentile, whether they were accepted by the other religious communities and culture around them or were being persecuted—all kinds of things.

And so all the Gospels are like that? Written from a particular point of view to make sense of the Christian faith depending on their own questions, situations, and struggles?

I think so. Which casts a totally different light on the differences we noticed earlier. The Gospel writers are each telling the story differently in order to make a different point, to answer a different question, to respond to different situations and challenges of their distinct communities.

Then it seems silly to regard these differences as "mistakes" that you have to explain away or defend. They're just different ways to tell the story of Jesus so people will believe that the gospel makes sense and is relevant for them.

That's right. More than that, these differences give us insight into what's at stake for these different writers. They give us clues into the nature of each Gospel writer's confession of faith.

That's an interesting point. Can you give me an example?

Absolutely. For instance, Jesus' best-known sermon is . . .

The Sermon on the Mount.

Right, except that in Luke's story Jesus isn't preaching on a mountain, he's preaching on a plain.

The Sermon on the Plain? Doesn't have quite the same ring. Where does "mount" come from?

That's in Matthew's version.

Now, one way to deal with this kind of difference is to ask, "Which one got it right?" and then argue about it. Another way is to try to explain away the difference by saying something like, "Well, obviously Jesus offered this sermon twice, once on a mountain and once on a plain, and the evangelists were reporting different sermons."

Frankly, neither of those responses seems that productive. In the first, how could you tell which version was right, anyway? And even if you think you know who got it right, does that mean the other story is less valuable, or even wrong? And the second way—explaining differences away—seems to miss the whole point.

By the way, what was the point of this difference?

Matthew, as I mentioned a little earlier, strongly links the story of Jesus to the story of Israel. He's most likely writing for a group of Jewish Christians who believe Jesus is the promised Messiah. That's why he begins, as we noted, with a genealogy linking Jesus to David, Israel's greatest king, and Abraham, the patriarch of Israel. At other places in his Gospel, Matthew points out how Jesus fulfills Old Testament prophecy. By setting Jesus' preaching of this sermon on a mountain, he's offering another link to Israel, by comparing Jesus and his sermon to Moses and the giving of the Ten Commandments on Mount Sinai. It's probably no accident, by the way, that in this sermon Jesus regularly reinterprets the law, the Torah, given by God through Moses.

Matthew will use this comparison to Moses again, in fact, to structure his whole picture of Jesus' teaching. He groups all of Jesus' teaching into five parts, which correspond with the first five books of the Bible, also known as the Pentateuch. These five books are traditionally associated with Moses. In a sense, Matthew is confessing the faith of his community that Jesus is a new Moses.

Wow. I never knew any of that, but I can see how it makes a big difference in reading and understanding Matthew's Gospel.

Which is why paying attention to these differences is so important. Whenever you stumble upon one of these differences, the question to ask is never, "Which one is right?" but instead, "What is this writer trying to say, trying to confess, with this detail?" Far from being threatening, these differences give you incredible insight into the nature, purpose, and meaning of that writer's distinct confession of faith.

Like John having Jesus die on the afternoon of the day before Passover, when the Passover lambs are sacrificed, because John is confessing that Jesus is the Passover lamb.

Exactly.

And have we only noticed these differences recently? I mean, is that why people are so upset now and have all these theories explaining away the differences?

No. The early church, while also believing the Bible was inspired, was keenly aware of the differences. And sometimes it caused some problems. Even though people in the ancient world didn't link facts and truth the way we do, they certainly had a sense that different witnesses to the same event could be pretty confusing to people wanting to find out about Christianity, especially when the different account disagreed on major details.

For this reason, one of the early leaders of the Christian church, a man by the name of Tatian, who lived around the middle of the second century, actually combined the four Gospels into one version, smoothing out the differences into a harmonious whole.

So what happened to Tatian's version? I've never heard of it.

For several centuries, it was pretty popular in Syria, the region where he lived and worked. But eventually most Christian communities continued reading the four distinct Gospels. I think they decided that they were better off with four separate Gospels, even with the differences between them.

They weren't concerned any more about confusion?

Well, they probably were concerned, but they felt that, on the whole, the truth about Jesus was too deep, too rich to be captured in any single portrait. So they lived with the occasional confusion four versions created because, taken together, those four Gospels offered a more complete picture of the truth about Jesus than any of them could offer alone or even a harmonized version of all four could offer. I think they realized that when you harmonized the Gospels, you lost the distinct confession of the Gospel writers, and what believers then and now really need isn't a summary of details but a living confession of faith.

So if they decided that four Gospels made for a more complete picture, why not five, or six, or more? What happened to the other Gospels?

That's a complicated question. Essentially, over time, as the church grew and expanded, its teaching about Jesus also grew and expanded, until there were a lot of different, sometimes very different, ideas about Jesus floating around.

Like . . .?

Like that he wasn't really human, but only looked that way because he was an angel in disguise. Or that he wasn't really born the Messiah, but was a mortal God chose, or adopted, to be the Messiah. All kinds of things—some pretty far out.

Eventually the church came to consensus that the four Gospels we have were the ones that offered the best or most helpful pictures of Jesus.

Is this what happened at the Council of Nicea? I read about that in *The DaVinci Code*. Dan Brown seems to think that the decisions about what books

to keep in the Bible were based on their prejudice about Mary Magdalene and women in general.

> *The DaVinci Code* was a great page-turner of a mystery novel, but not so great on history. The collection of books that make up our New Testament was never approved by any council. In fact, there are lists of the books in the Bible a lot like our own that date back to the middle of the second century, more than 200 years before the Council of Nicea took place. When it comes to the Gospels, it's significant that Tatian tried to harmonize the four we know about but no others.

Because even as early as Tatian, those were the four everyone thought were *the* Gospels?

> Exactly. None of these early lists are identical to ours. But most agree on the four Gospels, Acts, and the letters of Paul. Eventually, in 367 CE, a bishop by the name of Athanasius lists the 27 books comprising the New Testament in an Easter letter he writes to his congregations, but he's essentially confirming what had already been a long-standing practice in the church.

Wait a second. No council approved the list of accepted books? But what about Brown's conspiracy theory?

> Well, let's not forget Brown's book is a work of fiction.

But he says all the incidents and historical matters are accurate.

> He's also the guy who says he's championing the "feminine divine" but has only two female characters in his long book, an old lady who gets killed after a page-and-a-half and the love interest of the book's male hero.

Interesting. Okay, let's get back to how the New Testament was put together. If the church, or Athanasius, or whoever, collected some books but left others out, what did they base their decisions on?

> Usually three criteria. The first was that each book had to be associated, directly or indirectly, with one of the original apostles.

But wasn't Thomas a disciple?

Yes, although it's doubtful whether the disciple Thomas actually wrote that Gospel.

Really? You mean it was a forgery?

Yes and no. Yes, in that people sometimes intentionally wrote in another person's name. No, in the sense that the ancient world didn't have quite the same practices that we do. It actually wasn't that uncommon to write and publish in someone else's name. Sometimes that was because you wanted people to buy your book, thinking it was by someone they trusted. This is probably closest to our sense of forgery. But other times you wrote under someone else's name because you were trying to write in the same spirit of the original author. In a sense, by borrowing someone else's name, you were borrowing their authorization.

So the first criterion wasn't exactly ironclad.

No, and that didn't trouble anyone. The books just need to be associated with one of the early apostles, not necessarily written by them.

So what was the second criterion?

This one mattered a lot more, actually, and it was really pretty simple. The Gospels that made it into the Bible were the ones that most Christian communities were still reading.

Huh?

They were the ones that, a century or more after they were written, many different congregations still found useful. Many of the other Gospels floated around, sometimes coming in and out of vogue for a while in a particular region. But over time the churches largely stopped reading them. Eventually, the four we have were the ones that most Christians were still reading, the ones judged to be helpful not just in one region or another but to the whole church.

So it was a popularity contest?

Hmm, not so much a popularity contest as much as an endurance test. Over time, folks just stopped reading books that didn't seem that helpful. It's not unlike what happens today. The books we call classics are the ones that stand the test of time, the ones we think are worth handing on to our children and teaching in our schools. There's no single panel that gets to decide what book gets to be called a "classic." It's more that over time, all kinds of people, from the literature professor to the everyday reader, keep finding something worth thinking and talking about in *Huck Finn*, *Little Women*, or *King Lear*.

That's not quite as juicy as Dan Brown's account.

Well, there certainly were controversies. John's Gospel, for instance, at many points seemed a little too close for comfort to some teachings the church had declared were heresy. Which brings us to the third criterion: that the books in the Bible had to teach the orthodox faith.

"Orthodox"?

Orthodox literally means "right praise," but we might think about it more as teaching the "right doctrine." The opposite of orthodoxy is heresy.

Got it. Well, this criterion sounds more like Brown's conspiracy theory.

Except that what was considered orthodox was being figured out at about the same time the discussions about what books should be in the Bible were taking place. Sometimes it's hard, in fact, to figure out if certain books made it into the Bible because they were orthodox or whether we decided what was orthodox because of what the books people regarded as Scripture were saying.

This is definitely what happened in the case of the Nicene Creed that was hammered out at the Council of Nicea.

What do you mean?

The whole huge question of whether Jesus was human or divine led to an even closer reading of the different Gospels. So in Luke it was read that as a boy, Jesus "grew in stature and wisdom," which sounds pretty human, while in John it was read that "in the beginning was the Word, and the Word was with God, and the Word was God," which sounds pretty divine. So, the early church wonders—which is it, human or divine?

And they end up saying, essentially, "both."

Yup. The Nicene Creed is absolutely a compromise document, less defining of what Jesus is once and for all and more laying out the boundaries of all the different things you can say about Jesus without going too far in any one direction.

This sounds a little complicated.

It is, and probably is better left to another conversation. For now, the more relevant point is that questions about what books ought to be in the Bible was being decided at the same time all these other questions were being hashed out, and more often than not, this took place at the grassroots level of decisions that lots of individual congregations were making rather than by any top-down decision-making structure such as an official church council.

And Dan Brown?

Well, I think that Dan Brown, ultimately, was interested in telling a great mystery that would sell a lot of books. And scandals and conspiracies typically sell a lot better than ordinary history.

Okay, so let's back up a bit. I can definitely understand that the answer to my question of who wrote the Bible is pretty complicated, but is there anything more definitive we can say? I mean, how much do we know?

It is very hard to say with confidence who actually wrote all the individual books, and even when we know who wrote them, we often don't know all that much about them. So maybe a better way to go about it is to ask, instead, "How did the Bible come about?" And that's something we know more about.

For instance?

A lot of the stories in the Bible were originally told orally—in the Old Testament perhaps for many generations—before being written down. And different oral, and sometimes even written, traditions were often combined in producing individual books. Eventually those books were combined into collections. Decisions about which books should be collected and read together and which of those collections should be considered Scripture—that is, authoritative for the faith communities reading them—didn't happen all at once.

In the Old Testament, the first five books, the ones associated with Moses and called the Pentateuch, were probably collected and considered authoritative around 400 B.C.E. The section of books containing what we call the histories—Joshua through 2 Kings—and the prophets were probably considered Scripture around 200 B.C.E. And the third part, called the writings, was not widely accepted as authoritative until around 90 C.E., nearly 60 years after Jesus' death.

That's a long process.

Yes, it is. And the New Testament had a similar, if more compressed, history, ranging over about 50 years, with the letters of the apostle Paul coming the earliest, in the early fifties.

Not the Gospels?

No, they are written later: Mark probably around 70 C.E., Luke and Matthew around 80, and John a little later, probably in the early 90s.

How do we know this?

All of these dates, of course, are guesses, but educated ones. Luke, after all, tells us he's not an eyewitness. And then there are certain references to historical events—like the destruction of the temple—that give clues to what was going on in the world as the evangelists were writing.

Who, or what, are the "evangelists"?

Sorry, that's another name for someone who writes a Gospel.

Okay, thanks. So you were saying.

Right. That by reading closely you can find clues about what was going on when the evangelists were writing. At some points, you can even tell that different evangelists borrow from each other or share some of the same sources and traditions. All of this literary detective work also helps us develop a pretty good idea of when different books were written.

The Gospels used some of the same sources?

We've gotten glimpses of that earlier, for example, when Luke and
Matthew have a common story of Jesus' preaching in mind but retell
it with different details in order to make different points. By reading
the Gospels carefully, scholars have suggested that Matthew, Mark,
and Luke are each unique works of art that draw from at least four
different traditions or sources.

What are they?

The oldest one is Mark's Gospel, as we just mentioned, which both
Luke and Matthew borrow from heavily. Most of Mark shows up in
Matthew, nearly verbatim in parts. And much of Mark is in Luke as
well, though Luke uses some of Mark's material differently. Matthew
and Luke also share a lot of other stories, mostly parables, that neither Mark nor John have, and so folks imagine there may have been
a separate source, probably a collection of Jesus' teachings. Scholars
call this source that Matthew and Luke shared "Q," from *Quelle*, the
German word for "source."

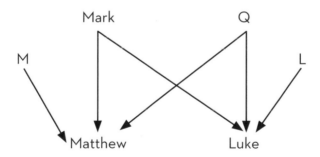

Very imaginative. And the other two sources?

Matthew and Luke each also have material unique to their Gospels,
such as the different accounts of the birth of Jesus.

**The Christmas story? Shepherds, angels, magi—I always think of that as one
story.**

We've heard the Christmas stories read and told so often we tend to unconsciously harmonize them, just like Tatian did with the whole New Testament. But they're really quite different. In Matthew's story, the angel Gabriel comes to Joseph, the descendant of David.

Given what we've said about Matthew's concern to stress Jesus as the Jewish Messiah, that makes sense.

Right. And Matthew is also the one who tells us about the magi and the flight to Egypt. In Luke's story, though, Mary is the main character. And it's from Luke that we have stories about angels and shepherds. Each author is retelling the story of Jesus' birth to make particular theological claims that when, taken together, offer greater insight into the significance of Jesus' birth, what we now call the Christmas story.

So in addition to Mark and Q, it sounds as if Matthew had some additional materials or traditions to draw from, as did Luke.

That's right. And much the same occurs in the Old Testament, though there it's even more complicated, as different sources are woven throughout the major books.

Really? How do they know which is which? I mean, whenever I've heard it, it sounds like one story.

That's true to a point, although when you read more carefully you will notice differences in the plot or story that seem a little funny, or lines or pieces of a story that get repeated, but with slightly different emphasis

For instance?

Well, consider the creation accounts in Genesis.

Accounts? In the plural?

Exactly my point. In Genesis 1, there's one story of creation that begins with perhaps the most famous line in literature, "In the beginning when God created the heavens and the earth, the earth was a formless void." It's the story of God's creating the world in six days and resting on the seventh. In Genesis 2 and 3, there's a second account, though, that starts out differently:

> *In the day that the LORD God made the earth and the heavens, when*
> *no plant of the field was yet in the earth and no herb of the field had yet*
> *sprung up—for the LORD God had not caused it to rain upon the earth,*
> *and there was no one to till the ground; but a stream would rise from*
> *the earth, and water the whole face of the ground—then the LORD God*
> *formed man from the dust of the ground, and breathed into his nostrils*
> *the breath of life; and the man became a living being. And the LORD God*
> *planted a garden in Eden, in the east; and there he put the man whom he*
> *had formed. (Genesis 2:4-8)*

The story of Adam and Eve and the Garden of Eden?

That's the one. Interestingly, in the Genesis 1 account, God creates humans—male and female together—on the sixth day as the crown of creation. In the Genesis 2–3 account, God creates Adam, the first human, on the first day and then Eve later in response to Adam's need for a fit partner.

And it didn't bother anyone that there are these two stories, with different orders of how things happened?

Has it ever bothered you?

To tell you the truth, I never noticed. I think I just always put them together in my head and smoothed out any differences.

Most of us do that, unconsciously harmonizing differences, whether it's the creation story or the accounts of Jesus' birth or death. What do you think now that you have noticed the differences?

To be honest, I can't say it bothers me now as much as it makes me curious. I mean, so what was going on in each account? What was the point of the differences, the distinct confession of faith?

Congratulations! These are exactly the questions biblical scholars ask.

I don't exactly think I qualify as a biblical scholar.

You may be closer than you think, at least in the sense that these are the questions any good student of the Bible asks, and all you need to be a good student of the Bible is a little bit of faith and a lot of curiosity.

That I've got.

Okay then, so what do you think is going on in the two stories?

Well, I think they're trying to answer different questions, make distinct confessions of faith. The first one is concerned with how the whole cosmos came into being and seems to be confessing that God is the one who brings order out of chaos. And the second story seems more interested in humans, where we came from, why we're the way we are. This is the one, after all, that tells about the temptation and fall, right?

That's right, and I think you're also right in suggesting that each of the creation accounts has a different focus or question it's trying to ask.

So is this the way biblical scholars trace out different traditions, by noticing these kinds of differences?

Often it's just like that. Sometimes the differences are in plot or storyline. Sometimes they are more in literary style. Sometimes it's a different focus, as in Matthew's and Luke's distinct nativity accounts. Sometimes it's different key words. For instance, in many sections of the Old Testament, the author always refers to God by the name *Elohim*, while other parts use the name *Yahweh*. These different names for God give us clues about two different traditions that at some point were woven together in the books of the Bible we have.

Boy, it's kind of hard to hold onto a "fallen from heaven" sense of the Bible when you talk about it this way.

Is that troubling to you?

You know, not really. I find it all really interesting—the combining of different traditions or sources into various books, the editing and collecting of the books that seem most helpful. It's fascinating.

I think so too.

And I actually think it helps me hear what the writers were trying to say—to understand what I think you called their distinct confessions. But it does make it harder to think about the Bible being inspired, doesn't it?

How come? As we said before, all these different traditions, writers, and books have two things in common. First, they're all about God and God's relationship with humanity. Second, they're all essentially confessions of faith of people who were, quite literally, inspired by God to tell, write, edit, and collect these confessions into one great book of faith. In this sense, I think the Bible—and the process that gave us the Bible—is inspired. That is, I think the Holy Spirit was at work throughout this process. Not by dictating to people what to write, but by working in their lives to inspire them to share their faith.

So it's not the divine reference book that fell from heaven, but it's still a holy book, and God continues to work through it.

Exactly.

That helps. That inspiration didn't have to be in one single moment, like a lightning bolt from heaven, but could be spread throughout the whole process, even if it was at times a complicated and even messy process.

According to the Bible, that's how God regularly works: through complicated, even messy processes. Why? Precisely because the humans God works through—the same humans God loves, let's not forget—are also somewhat complicated and even messy.

More like "*often* complicated and very messy"—at least the humans I know!

Of course, when you look at it this way, the process didn't stop with the writing of any single book or even the whole Bible.

No?

In a sense, we can see God at work whenever people try to make sense of the story of God in order to draw people into relationship with God.

Which means, of course, that the Holy Spirit isn't done inspiring.

How so?

Well, I'd say that when a pastor preaches a really good sermon that brings the biblical story to life, the Holy Spirit is at work inspiring both the preacher and the listener. And in a good Bible study, as people learn more about God's love for them and the world, the Holy Spirit's at work inspiring the people gathered around the Bible. Or when you or I tell someone else about how the story of faith in the Bible helps us make sense of our lives, the Holy Spirit is still at work inspiring our words and the person who hears them.

You mean to say that the words I hear on Sunday—or might even say to someone else—could be *inspired*?!

Perhaps not in quite the same way the Bible is inspired. After all, those words have been around for thousands of years and have stood the test of time. They hold the normative stories of faith that bind all Christians together. But could God be at work in your words and actions to make the same story come alive today? Could God be "inspiring" your witness? Absolutely.

That's something I've got to give some thought to. It's just a little bigger, more dynamic way of thinking about God being at work in the Bible and our world than I'd imagined.

Take your time. It's definitely worth thinking about.

Insights and Questions

CHAPTER 5

How Can I Read the Bible with Greater Understanding?

So, I've been thinking a little more about what you said about being a student of the Bible.

> And . . . ?

And I think I like that idea. I'm finding that the more I learn about the Bible as a book of faith, the more it makes sense to me, the more it seems actually relevant to me, as if it has something to say worth listening to.

> That's really great.
> I think a lot of people find that when they're freed to really use their minds to think about the Bible as a book, a human book that God uses to achieve divine ends, it actually becomes more important to them.

I know. Seems like folks who read it as a divine reference book fear the opposite will happen. You know, the more you stress its human quality, the less important it is. But I'm finding the opposite. It's like I can take it more seriously because it's not magical, but real, so it can speak to the real person I am and the real issues I have.

Karl Barth, a Swiss theologian who was perhaps the greatest theologian of the 20th century, once said that he took the Bible far too seriously to read it literally.

That's what I'm finding too. But there's a problem.

What's that?

Well, to be honest, I find reading the Bible a somewhat confusing experience. There's a lot in it that I'm not familiar with, a lot that doesn't totally make sense to me, and I'm not always sure what a passage means when I read it.

I don't think you're alone in that. And I definitely don't think you should feel bad. After all, the Bible was written 2,000 to 3,000 years ago, in cultures very different from our own, and in writing styles we don't often see anywhere else. So there's a lot that's foreign about the Bible, and that can make reading it challenging.

But the good news is that there are a few principles of biblical interpretation that aren't that hard to learn to help you in your reading.

I was hoping you'd say that!

Well, I wouldn't want to disappoint!

Okay, so the field of study we're entering into is usually called biblical criticism.

Whoa—wait a second. I said I wanted to read the Bible, not belittle it!

What? Oh, you mean the term *criticism*.

Yeah. Criticizing the Bible doesn't sound like something good Christians should do.

I see what you mean. The thing is, while we often use *criticism* to mean "saying not very nice things," it also means, "to study carefully." And "biblical criticism" is essentially a synonym for "biblical interpretation."

Maybe. But it still doesn't sound very friendly.

Well, try this for a minute: have you ever read a review of a movie before going to see it?

Sure. I especially like seeing what Roger Ebert has to say. He's really good.

And do you know what Roger Ebert's job title is?

Yes, he's a . . .
Okay, I get it—he's a film critic.

Right. And he doesn't write his reviews to belittle the films he watches or because he doesn't like movies.

Of course not—he loves movies, and he writes his reviews to help movie-goers like me get more out of their experience.

Exactly. Biblical criticism functions the same way. The biblical scholar—or biblical critic—studies the Bible carefully because she or he loves the Bible, wants to read and understand it better, and wants to help others do the same.

Okay, that helps. Thanks.
So, you were saying there are a couple of principles of biblical criticism— it's still going to take a little getting used to saying that!—that we should know about.

Right. In particular, keeping two things in mind will help. First, reading the Bible on your own is good, but reading it with others is better.

Why is that?

The Bible, when you think about it, is a very communal book. It was written by lots of different people, usually with a community in mind. It's been collected, handed down, and interpreted by communities, and it tells a communal story, the story of what it means to be part of the family of God.

When you read it with others you come closer, I think, to realizing its intention—to build a community of faith around its confession of the God who is out to be in relationship with a community, the community we call "humanity."

So is reading the Bible on your own wrong?

Absolutely not! It's great to read the Bible on your own, whether for devotions or study. But you may discover that you get more out of it, have a better understanding of it, and enjoy it more by reading it with others. Like I said, it's very much a community-oriented book.

Which is probably why our pastor is always promoting Bible studies at church.

Probably.

Okay, I'm starting to think I should give going to one of those Bible studies a little more thought.
And the second thing to know about reading the Bible?

That being a student of Scripture is a little bit like being a detective.

Cool. I love C.S.I.

Well, hopefully Bible study will be just as intriguing but a little less gruesome. At least, I hope we don't end up at the morgue.

Seriously, though, I have a feeling I know where you may be going with this one.
When you don't understand a passage, you have to look for clues and put them together to understand what it's really saying. Like we did with the cre-ation accounts or with the differences in the way Matthew and Luke describe Jesus' Sermon on the Mount . . . or Plain, depending on which one you're reading!

Very good! Because the Bible is an ancient document, there are a lot of things we just don't know about it, and sometimes that includes its context. So you've got to look for clues that fill in what's missing. A good detective puts the clues together to solve a mystery, and a good student of the Bible does the same to piece together the author's con-fession of faith.

There's another way that reading the Bible is like solving a mys-tery too.

Yes?

Any good detective has a number of different tools to surface good clues. Sometimes it's physical evidence like a footprint, and sometimes it's testimony from a witness. Sometimes it's forensic evidence, while at still other times it's a pattern of events that suggest a certain solution. A good detective chooses which tools to employ based on the nature and circumstances of the mystery. And sometimes you just have to try whatever methods you have until you find a clue that leads you to the solution.

Reading the Bible can be like that too. You employ different techniques based on the kind of passage you're dealing with, and sometimes you have to keep trying until you find the one that yields a good reading.

I'm guessing biblical scholars don't often find footprints, so what kinds of tools do they use?

Well, one tool that's been very helpful has been archeology—you know, studying ancient sites where people in the Bible lived to get a sense of what their culture was like. And that is, actually, a little like looking for footprints.

But, you're right, finding physical evidence isn't a possibility for most of us, so thankfully there are lots of other methods, most of which you can use without leaving the comfort of your own home. You mentioned one just a moment ago—comparing the way two authors describe the same scene. So noticing that Matthew describes Jesus giving his sermon on a mountain, instead of on a plain as in Luke's account, offers a clue to Matthew's larger confession of faith. Comparing the way two authors use a common tradition, story, or source, is called *redaction criticism.*

It's called what?

Redaction criticism. A "redactor" is a fancy name for an editor. So it's really asking the question of what the biblical authors did with material they received and why they did it. In what way were they functioning as an editor, and what does that tell us about their distinct confession of faith?

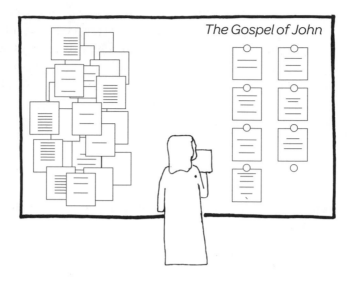

Redaction criticism tries to determine what the writers and editors did with the material they received and why.

Like when John says there were lots of stories he didn't use, it makes you pay attention to the ones he did.

Exactly.

This is just one way of approaching the passage. There are lots of others, and none of them will ever do the job every time, so like a good detective, you choose your tool, or exegetical method, depending on what you're dealing with.

Okay, hold on. Time to call in the "big-word police"—exa-what??

Sorry. *Exegetical.* It comes from the word *exegesis,* which comes from the Greek language and means literally "to lead out." It's used to describe methods that help you "lead out" the meaning of a passage. Think of it as a synonym for "interpretation."

exegesis

Exegesis describes what happens to "lead out" the meaning of a passage. It guides our interpretation.

Right—so between "biblical criticism" and "exegetical methods," I feel like I'm gaining a new vocabulary.

Well, any disciplined method of study does have its own jargon, which can be helpful to summarize things, but we'll try to keep it at a minimum. And when I forget and introduce a new term, feel free to keep letting me know.

Don't worry, I will.
Alright. So it sounds like exegesis is pretty important?

It's very important, because it helps you hear the biblical passage on its own terms. The temptation in reading anything that is different or challenging is to gloss over those differences and read our own biases into them. You can't *completely* rule out your own biases, but you can at least give the biblical passage you're reading a better hearing by employing a disciplined method—a method that forces you to focus on an element of the biblical passage you're reading rather than on your own preconceived notions.

For instance . . . ?

A number of the exegetical methods we're going to look at share a common concern: they want to put the passage we're reading into its historical context.

Why historical?

So we can better understand what it meant to the original readers. And that helps us discover its meaning today.

How does that work?

Well, in this sense, reading the Bible is a little bit like buying real estate.

Huh?

Ever heard what the three most important words in real estate are?

Sure—location, location, location.

Right. Well, the same is very much true in biblical study. The location, or context, of the passage you're reading is incredibly important.

Usually, you get at that by asking questions.

Who was the original audience this document was written for?

What were their circumstances?

What was the author trying to accomplish?

What comes before and after the passage you're reading?

Is the passage you're reading a parable, a wisdom saying, a legal indictment, a word of comfort, a prophecy of woe?

And is it part of a narrative, like a Gospel; a letter, like those of Paul; a book of poetry or wisdom, like Psalms or Proverbs?

And so forth. By asking and answering these kinds of questions, you locate the passage in its historical and literary context and so are more likely to understand it correctly.

So, location, location, location or, a little more accurately, context, context, context are among the three most important words in biblical studies.

That makes sense. By putting the passage in its larger context, you're more likely to understand what the biblical writer was trying to say, was trying to confess.

Exactly.

And exegetical methods help you do that?

Right.

Were these invented by theologians, then?

Actually, you might say that they were invented to protect the Bible from theologians!

You're kidding, right?

Only partly. Exegetical methods were developed by scholars in all kinds of fields—literature, history, biblical studies, and so forth—to help gain a more objective reading of different texts—literary, historical, or biblical.

For much of the church's history, theologians tended to interpret the Bible along the lines of their own theological categories. Doing that made it harder to hear the distinct witness of the discrete passage you were reading. That's why after the Reformation and the Enlightenment, many biblical scholars embraced exegetical methods as a way, in fact, to "rescue" the Bible from the theologians.

So today we have a number of different exegetical methods to figure out what a biblical passage means. Why are there different ones? Is it because none of them will work every time and it's helpful to have a variety of tools at your disposal?

That's the idea.

But when you say there are "lots of ways" to read the Bible, are we talking about three or four ways, or thirty or forty?

Probably somewhere in between; so more like a dozen or two dozen.

Whew—that's a lot of stuff to learn. Do I have to go to graduate school first before I can read the Bible well?

Absolutely not. We can learn together right here how to read the Bible well.

Of course, reading and understanding the Bible is never a once-and-done thing. There's always more to learn, and some people do go to graduate school and, in fact, spend their whole lives studying the Bible. Just like some people go to school and spend their lives studying Shakespeare, movies, engineering, or any of a number of other things. And you can learn a lot from what biblical scholars study through the books they write. Many of them are intended for everyday readers.

But we can also learn a few of these methods ourselves and feel more comfortable in our own reading. It helps that many of these methods actually have a lot in common, so we can simplify things greatly by grouping them into about four different types, or schools, of exegetical tools.

That sounds a little more manageable.

So what we'll do is look at four ways to interpret the Bible according to four different places a reader of the Bible might look for the meaning of any given passage.

I'm not sure I'm following—places to look for its meaning?

Yes. Let me back up a little.

When you're reading a biblical passage—or almost any other kind of literature, for that matter—the most important question you ask is "What does this mean?" Actually, this is true in all forms of communication, because communication is essentially the way we share meaning.

Like we talked about when we discussed the Bible as the Word of God—whatever medium of communication we may use, we're essentially trying to share the meaning or significance of something.

Exactly. When it comes to the most common form of communication—everyday conversation—you barely notice you're asking this question because the meaning is easily apparent.

Although sometimes it's not—like when you ask, literally, "What did you mean?"

True. Even in everyday conversation we sometimes need to trace out the meaning of something. That becomes more difficult when it's writing, of course, because the author's not there. But, essentially, we're asking the same question: "What did you mean?"

And how do you answer that question?

Well, you've got some choices to make. Unlike a conversation, which is pretty immediate, a written document has a history. That history stretches from the original event that caused the writer to write something in the first place all the way to when you read it yourself. That means we can imagine a timeline from that original event to today's reading of the passage.

I'm still not sure I'm following.

Don't worry. We'll work with a number of examples.

That sounds like a very good idea.

The important thing for now is to imagine that every book in the Bible has a history, so we can imagine a timeline stretching from the moment something was said or done that caused someone to take notice all the way up to your reading or hearing a biblical passage, whether on Sunday morning in worship or in a Bible study, or even reading on your own.

Okay, I can keep that sense of the history of each book in mind.

All timelines mark various points of interest, some greater than others. So, if you're doing a timeline of the Revolutionary War, you might indicate all of the protests, events, and battles with little hatch marks, but for the really important moments—the Boston Tea Party, the signing of the Declaration of Independence, Washington crossing the Delaware, and so on—you'd use larger hatch marks, because each of them represents a turning point or a particularly significant moment.

Yeah, that makes sense. But how does this apply to the Bible?

The Bible's timeline is a lot bigger, since it stretches from things that happened a couple thousand years ago all the way up to today. But to keep things a little simpler, we'll look at four major stops on the timeline. These are the major hatch marks. You could choose to look at lots of smaller ones, but each of these major stops reflects a particular dimension or aspect of the Bible and its use.

Hmm. I think this would be a great time for one of your examples.

Sounds good. Let's get away from the Bible for a minute and look at something more familiar, like a piece of music.

What kind of music?

Any kind of music will work—jazz, rock, country, classical, whatever.

Really? I thought for sure you'd have me pick Handel's *Messiah* or something else you always hear in churches.

We can certainly use Handel if you want. But if that's not what you usually listen to, then pick a favorite.

I've always liked Johnny Cash's "Folsom Prison Blues."

Perfect. Let's use it. What we're after is the meaning of the song.

That's interesting, because now that you mention it, I don't usually think about what a song "means" per se, but rather just enjoy it.

That's true, and that's similar to a lot of our listening and reading, whether a favorite album or book or even the Bible. But at some level we're always *experiencing* the song we're listening to or story we're reading. And so we can talk about different ways it moves us, has an impact on us, and in this sense means something to us.

All right. Let's try it out on Johnny Cash.

Fine. So what I'm suggesting is that we can think about "Folsom Prison Blues" in at least four ways. We can think about the things that happened before Cash recorded the song that influenced how it came to be.

I know something about that. I believe he wrote it while he was in the Air Force. While stationed in Germany he saw a movie about Folsom Prison, and apparently it inspired him to imagine what life in prison would be like and eventually to write this song.

Exactly. So this first dimension deals with the history behind the song, everything that led up to it.

A second dimension deals with the song itself—its words, music, rhythm, and mood. Here you're looking at the song as a song, as a work of art, and letting it guide you in how to hear it.

Absolutely. When we say he wrote it in the Air Force, that gives us some interesting information, but in the end, doesn't tell us all that much about what it really means. Although . . .

Yes?

Well, it occurred to me that with some songs, knowing the story behind it makes a huge difference. Like when you find out that Thomas A. Dorsey wrote the gospel song "Precious Lord, Take My Hand" after his wife and newborn baby died. He never mentions that specifically in the song, but when you find that out it totally affects how you hear it.

Definitely. But not all songs are like that.

No. That's not the case with "Folsom Prison Blues," for instance. I mean, knowing the background is interesting, but it's only when you listen to it that you really experience it.

So in this case, the meaning isn't behind the song, as in "Precious Lord," but actually right there in the song. Because Johnny Cash is a talented songwriter and singer, he can share meaning with you right in the song itself without any story behind it.

Right.

And it doesn't stop there. Because part of the song's meaning is also wrapped up in its impact over the years—like what happened when it was released, how it affected future songs by Cash, how it influenced other musicians, how it's been listened to and interpreted in the years since it was released.

It's actually been in a couple of different collections. It was first released in 1955, but it became a big hit when it was part of a live album Cash did in 1968 at Folsom Prison. About two weeks after it was released as a single of that album, though, and just as it began climbing the charts, it was remixed and reissued without the line about killing a man because Bobby Kennedy had just been assassinated.

I didn't know that.

Yeah. Cash was against changing it at first, but there was no way producers were going to keep that line in right after Kennedy's death. It was just too upsetting for people.

But even the remix was a huge success, and ever since then it's been one of Cash's signature songs, showing up in several "greatest hits" collections. People have credited that song and album as capturing the "freight train sound," as well as helping to define what a live album should sound like.

So we've looked at what's "behind" the song, in terms of the history leading up to it, and what's "in" the song in terms of its music and lyrics. Now we're looking at all the stuff "around" the song. This surrounding stuff isn't so much about the song itself but the way the song has affected other things and the way this history of its effects and interpretation shapes the way we might hear it today.

Yeah. I can see how much of that history gets attached to certain songs and comes back to us when we're listening to it.
Well, that's three places. What about the fourth?

Out "in front" of the song is the fourth place we'll look. That is, what's going on in our own lives when we are listening to it.

No kidding. There are times when I hear the song and it doesn't make that much of an impact. But there are other times, such as when I feel trapped or overwhelmed by everything I have to do, and I play that song because it captures my feelings, makes me feel like I'm right there in that prison with him.

Listening to music or reading a book is often like that—depending on what's going on, you can hear something familiar in a totally new way.

So now we've got four places to look for meaning, and I've used four different prepositions to get at what they might tell us about the song:

1. We look *behind* the song for the history of its development and what that might tell us about it.
2. We look *in* the song itself to consider it as a work of art.
3. We look *around* the song to check out the history of how it was played, listened to, and interpreted.
4. And we look *in front of* the song to take seriously how what's going on in our lives influences how we hear it. And you can plot all four of these on a timeline that stretches from Cash's time in the Air Force right up to when you listened to the song last night.

Locating the meaning of something

BEHIND	IN	AROUND	IN FRONT OF
↓	↓	↓	↓
What is the historical situation that led to or affected its creation?	What does it actually say?	How has it been used and interpreted?	What is happening in our congregation, community, and world that affects how I read, listen to, or interpret it?

How'd you know I listened to it last night?

Just a lucky guess. I figured it came to your mind so quickly because you listened to it recently.

Pretty good!
So, I have to say that this actually makes a lot of sense. It's hard to pin down one exact "meaning" to this song, but I can imagine thinking about these different aspects of it and how each might affect how I hear the song at any particular time.

And you could do this with pretty much any well-loved song or book. Each of them has a history of development; an artistic shape; a history of use, impact, and interpretation; and each is heard or read in light of our present circumstances.

And this is what we're going to do with the Bible?

Exactly. We're going to look to these four places to help us figure out what any given Bible passage we're reading might mean.

I think I can imagine how that might work, but once again some examples would help.

Absolutely. We'll look at some different biblical passages both to gain a deeper understanding of these four places to look for meaning as well as to practice using them when interpreting the Bible.

125

Sounds good.

Okay, before diving in, though, I should clarify one more thing.

That sounds a little ominous.

It shouldn't be too bad, honest.

Essentially, I want to distinguish between the four places to look for meaning and a whole range of exegetical methods.

These aren't the same?

Not quite. There are all kinds of tools, or methods, to use for drawing meaning out of a biblical passage. And all of them could also be plotted on a timeline with their own little hatch marks. The trouble is, there are so many exegetical methods that it soon gets overwhelming.

Which is why we're condensing them into four?

Yes, but we're not looking at four particular methods, but at something more like four families, or schools, of methods that all share something in common.

For instance, there is no one historical method, but there are lots of exegetical methods that all take the history behind a text as their starting place.

Okay, I think I get it. The four places to look aren't methods themselves, but they are larger categories or families. We'll organize all the different methods into those families.

That's exactly right. Don't worry, this is something that will become more clear as we go.

I'll take your word on that.

In the meantime, if the "big-word police" will allow, I'll tell you the technical name for all this.

I think I can handle another technical word at this point.

What we're talking about is actually called *hermeneutics*, the study of how we interpret things. It's really the study of how we discover the meaning of, well, just about anything, although hermeneutics has usually dealt with literature, including biblical literature.

Each of the four schools of interpretation we'll look at has different convictions about where meaning is located on the timeline from the historical event that set things in motion all the way to our reading it today.

Okay. I'm more or less with you. And I'll trust it will fall into place more as we go forward.

Great. Okay, so let's start with the family of methods we'll call "historical," because they are all primarily convinced that the best way to understand the meaning of a passage is to discover the history behind it. Historians are interested in cause and effect, so they are trying to trace out the story of all the things that happened that led up to a certain event—in this case the writing of the book that you're reading.

Makes sense to me.

Not surprisingly, the major character in this cause-and-effect story is the original author. So one of the primary convictions of historical criticism is that the meaning of any passage is tied to its author and, therefore, one of the primary goals is to discover as much as we can the original intention of that author and the context in which the author wrote.

Again, makes perfect sense.

The challenge, of course, is figuring out what the author intended when a passage was written so long ago and the author, if we even know who the person was, is long dead.

So this is where the detective work comes in?

Right. And there are all kinds of clues, but since all of them lie behind the biblical book you're considering, the key to reading the Bible historically is to treat it like a window.

A window?

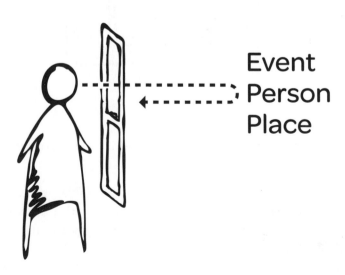

Event
Person
Place

Yes, in the sense that you're looking through the passage, trying to see behind it. You want to do that in order to figure out or discover some part of the passage's developmental history, something that may give you a clue to what the passage itself means. Let's look briefly at three examples.

The first is as close to pure history as possible. It's simply trying to discover as much as you can about the world of the author and audience. This is valuable in reading any biblical passage, but it's especially useful when dealing with material that is particularly contextual. The writing of a prophet trying to make sense of a particular event in Israel's history would be one example. A New Testament letter written to address a situation in a specific congregation would be another. With these kinds of works in particular, it helps to keep in mind the most important word in real estate.

"Location, location, location."

That totally makes sense. When we cleaned up my grandmother's house after she died, we found a bundle of letters in an old trunk in the attic. Different letters came from different times in her life: some she wrote home when she was in college; some were to her husband when he was in the war; others were to her children when they were grown; one very sad one was to her mother just after her youngest child died of a fever. Each of them had a particular context, and once we'd discovered that, they not only made a lot more sense, but also meant a lot more to us.

That's almost always the case with letters because they're so incredibly contextual. It helps a ton to know something about the author, the recipient, the circumstances in which the letter was written, the relationship between author and recipient, and the like.

A second example deals with particular literary forms, or genres, that shape the biblical passage we're reading.

Literary forms?

We have these in our own day too. When I say, "Once upon a time," you're pretty sure I'm . . .

. . . going to tell a fairy tale.

Which is very different from reading you a newspaper article.

Or if you're reading a document that begins with a date, then the address of the sender, followed by the address of the recipient . . .

I know it's a business letter, which is very different from a love letter.

Right. Well, the same thing is going on in different biblical passages. If you hear the words, "The Word of the Lord came to me," you can be pretty sure it's coming from a prophet. More specifically, if someone says, "Be not afraid," you know it's good news, and if it's, "Woe to you," you can be pretty sure . . .

. . . it's bad news.

Similarly, if Jesus begins a speech by saying, "The kingdom of God is like," you know . . .

. . . it's a parable.

Exactly. And parables, like prophetic utterances, fairy tales, and business letters are all distinct literary forms. Each has its own rules, and each conveys information in a different way.

So knowing the form helps you understand a passage better.

Right.

The third example of historical criticism I want to mention is one we've actually already looked at. It comes from comparing differences between authors who are covering essentially the same material.

Like the difference between Matthew and Luke around Jesus' birth or later in describing his sermon.

Exactly. And the key here . . .

I think I know—don't get bogged down in which one was right, but focus on what each one was trying to confess.

Right again.

Although you'd think a good historian would want to know just what happened.

Sometimes. But sometimes it's hard, or even impossible, to know for sure. And the reason this way of interpreting a passage is part of the historical family is that you're trying to figure out *why* Matthew described Jesus as preaching on a mountain rather than a plain—a decision that rests behind the text—so as to understand the meaning of that part of Matthew's Gospel.

Well, I have to say that, all in all, the historical family of methods has a lot going for it.

No question. In fact, for the last couple of centuries, it wasn't just one way to interpret a biblical passage. In many Protestant and Roman Catholic circles, it was the only way.

So what happened?

Well, a couple of things. First, the harder folks worked on figuring out the history behind a text, the more they realized that, often, you couldn't figure out that history—at least not in an absolutely certain kind of way. Lots of times there just isn't enough solid historical information to come to reliable conclusions. And if the only tools you have in your detective kit are historical ones, sometimes you come up short.

Second, after a while it felt more and more that if you weren't an expert in history, archeology, cultural anthropology, and the like, you had no business trying to interpret the Bible.

I was wondering about that. I mean, I find the historical information interesting and helpful, but I also know this is all stuff I'd have to research.

True. And there are a lot of helpful commentaries to help us read better. But it still made more and more people, including pastors, feel like biblical interpretation was the realm of experts and, like they say on television, we shouldn't "try this at home."

There's one more reason people began to look for other ways to interpret the Bible, and it's very similar to what you discovered when talking about "Folsom Prison Blues"—sometimes the history behind the song, or passage, doesn't tell you that much about what it means. And, again, if the only place you look is behind the text, and what you find behind it isn't that interesting, you're sort of stuck.

So that's when they started looking to these other places for meaning?

Yeah. Although people outside the church were quicker off the mark than biblical scholars.

Really?

Yup. You see, the same kind of discussion was going on at college campuses in literature departments where, for years, scholars also assumed history was the best way to understand any piece of literature. For instance, if you wanted to know what Hamlet meant, you tried to figure out as much as you could about the history behind the play.

So you'd want to know as much possible about what was going on in Shakespeare's life at the time or about the political situation or even the finances of the Globe Theatre? So whatever you could discover might give you insight into what went into writing the play. Right?

Exactly.

Well, eventually, some people, dealing with the same problems we named, got kind of fed up and made what seemed like a radical suggestion: if you want to know what Hamlet means, try reading Hamlet!

That does sound pretty radical.

Yeah, I know it sounds like common sense. But the point was that Shakespeare, Johnny Cash, and the biblical writers are all talented enough artists to convey their meaning right there in the work of art itself.

So the key here isn't to look behind the passage but, as you said before, to look for meaning right there in the passage itself.

Right. The focus isn't on the author but on the finished product, the book. Here, you're not treating the passage like a window but more like a painting or some other work of art, paying attention to the details right there on the canvas to guide you in your interpretation. In the case of a biblical passage, you pay attention to its literary, rather than historical, dimensions—things like plot, character development, dialogue, point of view, changes in language, imagery, symbolism, and so forth.

So, I feel an example coming on.

You're getting to know me pretty well!

So for instance, Luke regularly shifts between different literary styles at different parts of his Gospel.

Shifts styles?

Yes. He writes his introduction very much like any contemporary Greek historian would write. But when he gets to the announcements about, first, John the Baptist's birth and then, second, Jesus' birth, he shifts into a style very much like the well-known Greek translation of the Old Testament. He also includes with each announcement predications of the baby's future greatness.

Why did he do all that?

In the introduction, he's signaling that he's writing a history just like the histories written of other important people of the time. When he gets to the birth announcements, though, he wants to signal that this story picks up the Old Testament stories, so he makes it sound like the Greek Old Testament. Further, in both the Old Testament and in other first-century histories, it was common to describe the predictions of greatness that accompanied the birth of great persons.

So each change of style is a signal?

Exactly. And Luke is a master at this. Each time he changes style, it's almost as if Luke's trying to get our attention. So in the case of the birth announcements, it's as if he's making sure we realize that John and Jesus might begin with pretty humble origins, but what's happening in the story is just as important as the birth of a king or prophet. Why? Because, according to Luke, Jesus *is* a king *and* a prophet, though you wouldn't know it from the outside.

I see.

And we hear Luke's confession more clearly by paying attention to a shift of literary style, the same way we might notice a shift of tone in a favorite song or the background music or lighting in a movie. These are things that artists use to produce the effect they want, and looking behind the book, song, or movie isn't terribly important.

Cool.

Yeah, it is. Let me share one more example before moving on. This one comes from John's Gospel, and happens when Jesus is brought to the Roman governor Pilate for trial just before his crucifixion.

All the Gospels have a scene like this, but John goes into much greater detail about the setting, which is placed in two parts—inside Pilate's headquarters and just outside them. Jesus is sent into Pilate's headquarters, while the religious leaders who bring Jesus to Pilate stay outside. John describes Pilate going back and forth seven different times while he's trying to figure out what to do with this guy that he suspects is innocent.

Seven times?

Yeah. Now, imagine a movie of this scene, the way John describes it, and imagine fast-forwarding it. What would you see?

Pilate wavering back and forth.

Exactly. Here's Pilate, the most powerful man in first-century Palestine, wavering back and forth, unable to make a decision, but ultimately making one for the sake of political expediency.

It's as if John is trying to use him as an example to say that no matter how powerful you may be, you must still recognize who Jesus is and do something about it.

That's exactly right. A lot of John's Gospel, in fact, deals with different people who are encountered by Jesus and their various reactions to him. Some are confused, some believe and tell others, some deny him, and still others confess. In this case, Pilate doesn't want to have to take a side, but John is saying "to not decide is to decide—you're either for Jesus or you're against him, there's no fence-sitting allowed."

And I bet you could do archeological digs for about a hundred years all around Pilate's headquarters, and you'd never get this meaning.

Absolutely, because this meaning isn't tied to the actual historical place where Pilate worked. Rather, John makes his point by setting the scene in Pilate's headquarters.

Very cool. So I started as a big fan of the historical school of interpretation, but it sounds like the literary one is just plain better.

I don't actually think one is better than the other. It's just that some passages lend themselves to a more historical or a more literary approach.

Can you use them both in a passage?

Yes, and often both are used together. On the whole, when dealing with literature as diverse as the biblical witness, it's good to have options.

So we've looked *behind* the Bible and *in* it. That's two of the four places you said we'd look at. What are the other two places?

Let's get to them now.

The third place to look is the history of the use, impact, and interpretation of the biblical passage. It's essentially to ask the question of what's going on around the text and how this might shape our reading. Sometimes it involves knowing the history of interpretation of a passage. It can help us to know, for instance, how John Wesley or John Calvin might have interpreted a particular passage. Or how that passage has been treated in art or music. Take Jesus' parable of the prodigal son, for instance. Some painters portray the son as genuinely sorry for what he's done, while others portray him as being sneaky, even conniving, when he comes back to his father.

What do they base that on?

Well, in Luke's account, it says that he rehearses what he's going to say to his father. It says nothing, though, about his motives. So it might be that it occurs to him what he ought to say because he's made a mistake, or it might be that he thinks about what he should say in order to get back in his father's good graces. Looking at an artist's rendition of a biblical passage can absolutely shape how you read it.

That makes sense. Some of the Christmas carols we sing probably shape how I hear the Christmas story as much as the words the Bible writers actually use.

That's a great point. Because it's not just the way people have interpreted the passage over the years, but also what's going on around the reading of the passage right there in church that matters. In a sense, if we looked at the historical and literary dimensions earlier, we're really looking at the ecclesial dimension now.

"Ecclesial"?

Sorry, it essentially means "church."

What I mean is that, whatever else the Bible is—a historical document, great literature, and so forth—it's also been the church's book for 2,000 years. So, how the church has read and continues to read it makes a difference. For instance, you can read the same passage, Psalm 23 . . .

I know that one: "The Lord is my shepherd, I shall not want. He makes me lie down in green pastures; he leads me beside still waters."

Where did you learn this psalm?

It was my dad's favorite. We read it at his funeral.

It's a lot of people's favorite, which is why it's popular at funerals, and sometimes at weddings. And of course we hear it on some Sundays as part of the larger pattern of biblical readings a lot of churches use.

And each time, depending on what else is going on around the reading of Psalm 23 in the church service, you not only hear something different, but it actually means something different.

Yes, I think you can say that.

That sounds a little like the fourth place you mentioned earlier, looking at what's going on in our own lives.

That's true. Both the third and fourth places are, in a sense, out "in front" of the text, in that we're looking at things beyond either the historical or literary dimensions of the passage. But I want to distinguish between the times we're paying particular attention to how the church has read and interpreted a passage and all the things going on around it during the church service—like baptism, communion, an anniversary, or a funeral—and the things going on right in our own lives that shape our reading too.

Okay, and what would those kinds of more immediate things be?

They might be local things such as the particular problems of your local congregation, or they might be national or world events. After 9/11, for instance, you heard Psalm 46 in a lot of church services. That's the psalm that begins, "God is our refuge and strength, a very present help in trouble."

That sounds familiar.

It's the psalm that inspired Martin Luther to write his famous hymn "A Mighty Fortress Is Our God." Which is why, before 9/11, if you heard this psalm at all in church, it was probably once a year, on Reformation Sunday, the day many Protestant churches commemorate the Reformation.

But in light of the national tragedy, it took on new meaning. I see that. It was important to hear these words of comfort during all the loss and confusion.

Exactly. We might even say that it meant something different on September 12, 2001, than it did on September 10.

I have a feeling that this isn't that uncommon. I remember my pastor once preaching on something the apostle Paul wrote about all things working together for good for those who love God. It was a good sermon, but the company I worked for had just gone bankrupt, and I just couldn't see how this was working for good. The whole thing made me kind of mad at Paul, actually, and I remember wishing my pastor had maybe challenged what Paul was saying a little more.

We definitely hear passages differently depending on what's going on around us.

The funny thing was, though, that a friend of mine who was at church that day said it was the most comforting verse to hear right then. We were experiencing

the same crisis, but we heard the Bible passage in two very different ways. Which I guess is part of the reason for having more than one way to hear and interpret a biblical passage.

> Like we've said before, some methods work better with some passages than others, and with most passages it's helpful to have a couple of options to try to hear it in a meaningful way.

That's true, but I think there's something more to it too. It's that the meaning of even a single passage is just too big to be contained in any single interpretation. I know that's true of my favorite songs or favorite books. There's no way I could pin down only one thing that it really meant—there's just too much there.

> That's a fantastic way of putting it. One of the great poets of the twentieth century, T. S. Eliot, said something similar once when talking about one of his poems: "When I first wrote that poem," Eliot said, "only God and I knew what it meant. Now, only God knows!"

That definitely captures it! As important as the author is, it's like the meaning of a poem or book or song somehow exceeds the grasp of even the author.
I think that's because meaning is more than what someone once thought. It's what the passage makes me think about today. This is why we can't look only to the past. Meaning is as much about the future as it is about the past.

> Say more; I really like where you're going.

Well, when we talk about making sense of a passage, I think we usually mean figuring out what it meant. But even though that's important, I think it's just as important to talk about what it might still mean—what it might still do to people who hear it. To put it another way, as important as the past is in understanding a passage, I think meaning is also about the present and future. Otherwise, how could we say—as you did earlier—that God is still speaking to us through the Bible?

> I think you're absolutely right. Meaning arises from the interaction of a book and its reader, and is never simply the property of one or the other.

Which means there are all kinds of potential meanings for any one passage, as all kinds of readers in all kinds of circumstances might read it.

Again, you're probably right.

But all this raises a big question, maybe the million-dollar question.

Yes . . . ?

Well, I can see how useful it is to have all these different methods in helping figure out what a passage means, like a detective with lots of investigative tools. But what happens when different methods lead to different results? How do you know which one is right? Is there even a "right" interpretation? If there's not, then can a passage mean *anything*? I mean, what if all these different methods result in tons of different interpretations? How do we know which to choose?

Those are great—and huge!—questions and deserve some serious conversation. For now, let me suggest a couple of things briefly, and we'll see where that leads us.

Okay.

First, if we think about a passage of the Bible in terms more like a favorite song than a math problem, we'll realize that we can probably live without one absolute meaning. Those favorite songs or novels we keep listening to or reading again and again—over the years they can keep saying different and true things to us at different times of our lives. Well, the same passage or story from the Bible also has the capacity to say different and true things to us in light of our circumstances.

I can see that. It's certainly true of my favorite songs, movies, and books. In fact, one of the things that makes something great is that it gets a lot of people talking. But is there a limit? Can a movie, or even a passage from the Bible, mean just anything?

Well, that's the second thing I wanted to remind us of again: Reading the Bible on our own is good. Reading it in community is better.

Yeah, I remember talking about that.

Most of the time, interpreting a passage with the exegetical tools we've discussed will lead you to what seems like a pretty solid interpretation.

But not always. As we've already seen, no one exegetical method can tell us exactly what a passage means, and even using all the methods in the world can't do that. So with challenging passages, it really helps to see and hear what other people are thinking. Biblical commentaries are helpful in this way, not as the expert's definitive word, but as guides to help you toward a better interpretation. And it's also helpful to see what other people right now are saying. This is why church Bible studies can be so rewarding. Because while I might hear one thing because of my life experience or familiarity with the Bible . . .

. . . or lack thereof!

Or lack thereof, absolutely.

While I might hear one thing, other people will undoubtedly hear something different, and it's helpful to listen to what others hear. This can be a corrective for the highly individualistic reading and interpretation of Scripture that our culture seems prone to. It can also help steer us toward a better interpretation, for as with so many things, so also with biblical study—two heads are usually better than one. Of course, even this can't guarantee we'll ever get to the one and only right meaning of the passage—if such a thing even exists—but we'll probably get closer if we work at it together.

Besides all this, it's also just plain more interesting and a lot more fun to study the Bible with others, as we learn together not only more about the Bible but also more about each other.

That makes sense too. I really enjoy reading books, and although I usually just read them on my own, once or twice I've been a part of a book group. I got a lot out of hearing what other people thought.

But I'm still not sure this solves things.

What do you mean?

Well, we've said that the exegetical methods and hermeneutical families we've been looking at are great ways to open up Scripture so that it might speak to us in a new way. They not only point us toward what the passage meant but also what it might still mean, so it can speak to us today.

Right so far.

But we've also said we'll never arrive at just one meaning for all time. For the most part we can live with that. Even though these methods can't guarantee the "right" reading, they can at least help us toward "better" readings. And reading the Bible in community helps us even more.

Right again.

But you didn't sound totally confident that even this will always yield the best interpretation.

Well, I think it usually will, but it certainly doesn't guarantee the best reading. I mean, whole communities have been wrong in their interpretations of Scripture, as when many churches used the Bible to justify slavery in the United States a couple of centuries ago or to justify apartheid in South Africa a couple of decades ago.

So where do we go from here?

This is going to sound like an odd answer, but I'd say we go to theology.

But earlier you said that exegetical methods were intended, in part, to protect the Bible from theology, from reading our own biases and assumptions— including our theological biases and assumptions—into the Bible. You said that might make us miss its distinctive confession.

You're right. I did say that.

So what gives?

Well, in light of the many possible things any given passage of Scripture might mean, I think you need a sense of what the core witness, or central confession, of the Bible is so that you can interpret all of the Bible in light of that. And, at its best, that's what theology does— clarify our confessions, and the Bible's confessions, about God.

And do you think there is a core witness, a central confession in the Bible?

I do, and I think that's probably what we should turn to next.

Great. Let's get going.

Insights and Questions

CHAPTER 6
Is There a "Center" to Scripture?

Okay, so I'm a little confused. You just said that it will be helpful for us to put our finger on the "central confession" of Scripture, and that this is the task of theology. But earlier you said that the job of exegetical methods was to protect the Bible *from* theology.

I did, although I said I was half-joking, if you remember.

But only half. I remember you said that for much of the church's history theologians interpreted the Bible through theological categories that made it difficult to hear the distinct witness of any particular biblical passage.

Wow, you really were paying attention.

Yes, I was paying attention, and so I want to know what gives. My sense was that exegetical methods help us read the Bible more objectively so that we don't just read our own biases, including our theological biases, into whatever passage we're reading.

That's right.

So why now, suddenly, are we turning to theology?

That's a great question, but it may take a little while to answer.

No problem. I've got time, and I'm really interested in your answer. I think this is important.

I do too.

Let me offer three reasons why it's important to use theology to help us discover whether there is a "center" to the biblical story.

Okay.

First, the Bible has so many different kinds of literature, was written over so many centuries, and contains so many different opinions and theological convictions that it's important to ask what, exactly, holds it all together.

Wait a second. I thought we had already said that God holds it all together—that what all these different books and authors have in common is that they've all had some kind of encounter with God and want to share that experience with others.

You're absolutely right. But now it's time to say more clearly what we mean by that. What kind of God are they talking about? And how do we recognize that God at work in our life today? Are there places where we see God most clearly that may help us make sense of other parts? Whatever we believe is at the "center" of the Bible will very much influence the way we answer these questions.

Okay, that makes sense.

Second, exegetical methods *are* very important in screening out some of the biases and presuppositions we bring to reading the Bible. This is why it's worth learning how to use them. But each method we use also has its own biases.

Wait a second. How can a method have a bias?

Each method makes certain assumptions about things; for instance, about where meaning is located.

Like whether we should look behind the text to the cause-and-effect chain of events that resulted in a biblical book, or whether we should just read the book as a work of art.

Exactly. Those are two very different assumptions or biases about where to look for meaning. Every method is like this—it makes certain assumptions. So while each method rules out some biases, each one also introduces others.

Which is why it's helpful to use multiple methods.

True, but you'll still never get a perfectly neutral, perfectly objective reading of the Bible. And, truth be told, you wouldn't want to.

What do you mean? I thought we wanted to get beyond our biases.

Well, this is the third thing I wanted to say.

Yes, we want to avoid simply reading our cultural values, assumptions, and prejudices into the Bible so it simply tells us what we want to hear.

But, no, we don't want to get rid of those biases completely, because they're why we read the Bible in the first place.

Ah . . . my head is starting spin a little. I'm not sure I follow what you mean.

Initially we go to the Bible because something about it interests us, or because we hope it will shed light on something that's important to us, or because we have a particular question we hope it will answer or problem it might help us solve.

All these things—our interests, questions, and problems—are part of who we are. They come, in part, from our biases and presuppositions. These are the things that make us interested in reading the Bible in the first place. In this sense, we might speak of "fruitful" biases, those things that draw us to read Scripture.

So, just to make sure I'm hearing you correctly: are you saying that when we read the Bible, we should *not* try to be objective.
This is definitely not what I would have expected you to say.

Yes, we should try to be objective. But at the same time, we need to admit that, ultimately, we can't be completely objective. And that's not entirely a bad thing. I mean, no one goes through life as a *tabula rasa*, a blank slate. We come with all kinds of expectations, and these expectations (and biases and presuppositions) set the stage for meaningful interaction.

For instance, did you ever go on a blind date?

Well, umm, yes, but why on earth are you asking me that?

I bet whoever set you up on that blind date told you to be open and objective—and I bet you tried. But the thing is, before the blind date ever got started and no matter how open to the person you might have been, you still had biases, expectations, presuppositions about what a "good" blind date would be as opposed to a "bad" blind date, right?

Definitely.

And those expectations were crucial in helping you make sense of your experience.

I guess so, yes. I suppose my expectations helped me evaluate what we did, what I liked or didn't like about the person, and so forth.

So, was it a good or bad date?

Just kidding, that's none of my business.

The point is, we aren't completely neutral; we can't be completely neutral, and it would probably be pretty hard to get through life if we were completely neutral. We'd have no basis for making important judgments.

Maybe. But I still think we need to be careful not to let our biases run roughshod over the Bible.

Absolutely. But that's different than imagining that a particular method—or even a whole bunch of methods—can grant perfect objectivity and rule our biases out completely. In fact, it's just when we think we've attained a state of objectivity that we're most likely, I think, to fall prey to our own biases or be captured by our presuppositions simply because we can't admit they're even there.

So maybe the role of method isn't so much to eliminate our biases, but to identify them?

Okay. I think I know where you are going.

Well, if we know what our biases are, that can be a good thing. Our biases might make us search out something in the Bible in the first place. And if we understand our biases, we can be more careful about simply reading them into the Bible.

That's nicely put.

Okay, so those seem like three pretty good reasons for trying to come up with some kind of center to the biblical story. But where does theology come in?

Theology helps us to order all these biases we have about God, the world, and each other into a coherent confession of faith. Theology helps us make sense of all the different voices and opinions in Scripture, and it helps us decide the various different interpretations we might discover.

Sounds reasonable.

But here's the difference between what I'm talking about and what theologians did for so many years. What I'm asking us to do is to state our theological convictions clearly so that we can put them into conversation with the convictions of the Bible.

And this is what theology and exegetical methods help us do?

Right. Meaningful Bible study is very much like the conversation we're having right now. Any good conversation is a two-way street. I mean, if one only person does all the talking . . .

It makes for a pretty shallow relationship.

Exactly. So theology helps us clarify our convictions about God, life, and each other, while exegetical method helps us give the Bible an honest hearing. Together they make for a much livelier, honest, and meaningful conversation.

Okay, so I can see where theology is helpful in clarifying the faith convictions we bring to reading Scripture, but I'm not sure how this addresses our earlier question about how we deal with competing interpretations of Scripture.

Essentially, when there are several competing interpretations available to us, we judge them, in part, according to how they match up with our core theological confession.

But if we just choose the interpretation that matches our theology, how is this any different than what you said we should be avoiding?

The key is remembering this is a conversation. We come to Scripture with a set of expectations and biases about God, life, pretty much everything. We'll call this our core confession of faith or theological worldview. This serves as a kind of lens. We read the Bible through this lens. And, as we said, it'd be hard to make sense of the Bible without some kind of lens in the first place.

As we read, though, we don't just ask questions and get answers—that's more of a one-way street. We also at times have our questions called into question, just as in a real conversation, or get different answers than we imagined, or even get answers to questions we weren't even thinking about.

So while we read Scripture through our theological lens, as we read, Scripture in turn shapes that lens even more. Then we come back to reading the Bible the next time with a slightly different lens. And in our reading we have our lens, our confession, shaped once again.

It sounds kind of circular.

It is circular. In fact, theologians call this "the hermeneutical circle" in that this process of reading through a particular hermeneutical lens and having that lens shaped by our reading never ends.

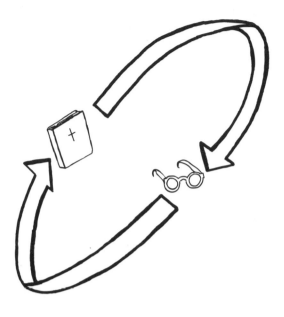

And this theological lens is what you've been calling the "center" of Scripture, the central confession of the Bible.

Yup.

And you get this lens from reading the Bible. I mean, it's not something totally outside the Bible?

Right again. Our life experience very much shapes this lens too. But not only does the Bible give us the primary images and stories about God that shape our theological lens, but the more we read the Bible, the sharper, or more accurate, that lens hopefully becomes.

Okay. That makes sense. But how do we go about figuring out what Scripture's central confession is?

That's the big question.

In short, I think that over time as we read the Bible we gravitate to the parts that seem the most clear to us; to the parts that seem the most important, both to us and to the story; and to the parts that shed the most light on our lives.

Over time, the particular passages, stories, or themes that seem most important to us and most central to the Bible tend to come together to form a worldview or set of core convictions about God, life, and the world. And in this way they form the lens through which we make sense not just of life but also of Scripture.

It really sounds like you're saying some parts of the Bible are more important than others, or at least that some parts become more important to us.

On one level, that's exactly what I'm saying. On another level, though, it's not so much about passages being important in their own right; it's more about how crucial they are to the biblical story and, in turn, to helping the biblical story make sense of our lives.

But I'm still not sure I'm comfortable with this. I mean, if the whole Bible is God's Word, shouldn't we pay attention to all of it?

By all means, let's pay attention to all of it. I'm just betting that some parts will seem more clear, more helpful, or more central to our understanding of God, the world, and each other—not to mention the Bible itself—than others.

And we should give those parts a higher place, honor them more?

It's not so much that we *should* give them a higher place, a place of privilege, but it's that we just *do*. In any story there are essential details and less essential ones. I'm suggesting we give more attention to the essential ones.

Think about it—when something really makes sense, or moves us, or helps us to make sense of the world, we return to those things again and again.

I know that's true with other books I've read, as well as with movies and favorite songs, but it feels a little different with the Bible.

Maybe. But I don't think it is. Whether it's a favorite book, a particular movie, or the Bible, we make sense of things by interpreting what's not clear in light of what is.

I think you're probably right. But I have to admit that I'm usually not aware that I'm doing that.

Don't worry, you're in good company. Most of us aren't aware of wearing any particular theological lenses any more than you're usually aware of wearing regular glasses. But, believe me, we all do. I mean, read through six months of your pastor's sermons and you'll soon have a pretty good idea what her theological lens is.

But my pastor doesn't preach the same thing every week. She's a really good preacher!

I'm sure she is, and part of what makes her good is probably a clear, compelling, and well thought out theological lens that helps her interpret all those passages she preaches on. This doesn't mean she says exactly the same thing each week, but over the weeks and months of her preaching, central themes and motifs probably keep coming up.

It's important to keep in mind that this isn't about good or bad. This is just the way it is. We can't help but interpret what seems less clear or even confusing through the lens of what we believe is clear.

This reminds me a little bit of my eighth grade social studies class.

Really? In what way?

That's where I learned about the Rosetta Stone. Do you know the story about that?

Isn't that the rock that helped crack the code of hieroglyphics?

That's it. Up until the stone was discovered, scholars had been unable to translate hieroglyphics, the picture-language of ancient Egypt. They had figured out bits and pieces but couldn't put it all together into a meaningful whole. Then they found this stone that had an inscription written in three languages, hieroglyphics and two others they already knew. By focusing on what they knew, they were able to figure out what they didn't know.

So it sounds as if you're suggesting we need a Rosetta Stone to understand the Bible.

I like that analogy. What we've been calling our "center" acts like an interpretive key for reading the whole Bible. By focusing on what's clear, we can make sense of what's less clear.

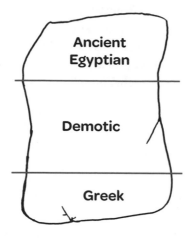

The Rosetta stone was used to learn how to translate difficult Egyptian hieroglyphics.

That helps me appreciate why we'd want to identify a center to Scripture. But I have to confess that it still makes me a little uncomfortable.

Why?

Well, even if we agree that we need to identify the clearest parts of the Bible over the others, who gets to decide what's central and what's not? That seems like a really big decision.

> It is a big decision. And it's something Christians have disagreed about for centuries. Essentially, key theological differences among the various Christian traditions can be traced back to differences about what the center of the biblical story is.

So are you saying Lutherans have one center, Presbyterians another, Methodists and Evangelicals their own, and so forth?

> Well, I don't want to give the impression that they're totally different. Most, if not all, of the Christian traditions that come from the Reformation, for instance, share a commitment to emphasizing God's grace over our response through good works. Most of these traditions would point to many of the same key passages, though in the end they would describe their "theological center" a little differently.

Are there some traditions that don't think we should have a center at all?

Actually, yes, I think you could say that some Christians believe they do not need an interpretive lens because they're just reading the Bible, plain and simple.

But it sounds like you don't think that's possible.

No, I don't. I think you are always reading from a particular point of view whether you realize you are or not. As I said about your pastor earlier, if we looked at six months of the sermons of *any* preacher, even one who denies having a theological lens, I bet we'd find that some passages, or theological themes, keep recurring.

The Bible is just too big and varied not to move toward certain unifying themes, significant passages, or central theological themes, and so we all end up with a theological lens through which we make sense of the whole Bible.

Sounds like you think this is pretty important.

I do, because when we're not honest about having a theological center, it becomes nearly impossible to talk with people who differ from us.

Why?

Well, simply this—if you can't admit your own bias, then you assume you've essentially got the truth.

Kind of like the bumper sticker I've seen: "The Bible says it. I believe it. That settles it."

Exactly. With that point of view, there's just not much to talk about.

So if you do admit you have a center, even that you need one, who gets to name it?

That's a great question, and it deserves a careful answer. So let me suggest four things that influence our belief about what's at the center of Scripture.

Okay.

First and foremost, one's theological center ought to come from reading the Bible. There's just no substitute for this. The more we read the Bible, the more we're in tune with its plot line and can discern its major themes.

That makes sense.

Second, as we've just been talking about, different Christian traditions are by and large defined by their primary convictions about the center of the Christian story. So the church you go to has been refining its sense of the center of the biblical story for centuries. If you listen carefully you'll pick that up in sermons and Bible study, and even in the favorite hymns that are sung again and again.

Hmm. Sermons make sense. But I guess the hymns you pick reflect the primary theology of the church too. Good. I'll be listening more carefully.

Great. Third, you and I each come to put into practice the theological priorities of the churches we're a part of based on our own experiences and convictions. So, even members of the same church may do that a little differently.

No kidding. I definitely see things differently than some of the folks in my congregation. But now that you mention it, they're probably minor differences in the larger picture, more like family squabbles than church-dividing issues.

Fourth, different times and situations sometimes call for different emphases. So the same Christian tradition may emphasize different elements of its theological inheritance to face new challenges. Lutherans, for instance, have always emphasized that we are justified by grace through faith. In Luther's day, when the dominant picture of God was that of a just and fierce judge, the Lutheran emphasis had a lot to say about whether one bought indulgences or not.

"Indulgences"?

Did you ever play Monopoly?

Sure.

Well, indulgences were sort of like a "get out of jail free" card that you could buy to reduce your time in purgatory, the place you paid your debt for sin before going to heaven. The medieval church used the money it raised from indulgences to build cathedrals and the like.

Buying down your sentence—doesn't sound totally fair to me. Do people still think you can purchase indulgences to get to heaven faster?

Most don't, and that's exactly the point. Today, not many people are paying money to reduce their time in purgatory. In fact, a lot of people don't worry about whether God is merciful or judgmental in general. But a lot of folks may be struggling to find a sense of identity or meaning in our world, so we may ask how "justification" responds to this question.

But shouldn't we think of the Bible as offering "timeless truth"?

Absolutely. And a lot of it too. Which means that we'll often emphasize certain parts in relation to the particular issues or crises of the day. We can keep going back to the Bible because it offers a complex enough story to help us make sense of a very complex world.

So, the Bible's truths are not only timeless but "timely."

Good way of putting it.

Thanks.

Okay, we construct a sense of the biblical center from these four primary places: the Bible, our church tradition, our individual experience, and the timely cultural issues of our day. And it's important to remember that this isn't once-and-done. Because if you really are reading and studying the Bible carefully, then you'll have to keep refining your sense of the Bible in light of what you're reading and hearing. It's a big book and has a lot to say, and as long as you're reading carefully, you'll keep hearing and learning new things. And some of them are bound to question and refine your theological lens.

Back to the hermeneutical circle. Which brings up another question: over time, does your theological lens keep improving, getting better and better?

One would hope so. But while it's easy to look back and see the mistakes made in previous generations—about slavery or the role of women, for instance—it's harder to see our own blind spots. And, truth be told, I think some of the earlier Christians probably had a better sense of how to respond to those who were poor than we do. So I'm not sure I'm quite ready to call it a "hermeneutical spiral," in the sense that we can guarantee that our interpretations will keep getting better.

But "circle" can feel a little repetitive. So how about the "hermeneutical Slinky"? As our interpretations hopefully get better, whether they're going up or down, the key is that we keep reading and listening to Scripture.

I like that, especially because a Slinky is dynamic, energetic, and just plain fun.

Thanks.

So I have to say that this is a lot to keep straight.

I know it can feel a little overwhelming. But what's most important is actually not trying to keep everything we've talked about straight, but remembering two key things. First, we *all* have a fruitful bias about what Scripture is really about—what we've been calling our "center" or "theological lens"—what you helpfully described as our "Rosetta Stone." Second, it helps us to articulate that center both for our own reading as well as talking with others about the Bible.

That's good, but I still think it would be really helpful if you could describe what you think the center of Scripture is, so we'd have a working example to look at.

No problem. Although I want to make clear that this remains a matter of confession. I mean, there's no neutral court of appeal that will render a verdict that this is going to be the best or most true center of them all.

I appreciate the disclaimer.

Well, I'm just trying to be honest, because the minute you think you've got it all figured out, you stop learning, and the conversation between you and the Bible, as well as the conversations you have with other Christians, gets dull really fast.

Fair enough. So where are you going to start?

How 'bout with Scripture.

I kinda figured that. But where?

No. I don't just mean in Scripture, but really start with Scripture, as in, let's pay attention to what Scripture itself values highly.

You mean the Bible already starts lifting up some of its passages as more central or important than others?

Absolutely.

There are certain scenes in the biblical drama that get referred to over and over again. In the Old Testament these include Israel's deliverance from Egypt and the giving of the law at Mount Sinai—we might call these the "Moses story"—and the reign of King David—we can call this the "David story."

That's right. I remember you mentioned earlier that there were two versions of the giving of the Ten Commandments.

Right. And both are tied to God's rescuing the Israelites from Egypt. Again and again in the coming years, the prophets will refer to these events as central to Israel's self-understanding, to their identity, and to their sense of what God is calling them to be and to do in the world.

And King David?

It's not just David himself, but the promise God makes to David that he and his descendants will rule over Israel forever. This is important not only in the Old Testament but also in the New, as the Gospel writers confess that Jesus is the promised heir of David.

What happens to the Moses story?

That's picked up in the New Testament as well. Earlier we looked at how Matthew structures his whole Gospel around the giving of the law at Sinai. In many ways, these two strands of the Old Testament, Moses and David, come together in the New Testament's portrayal of Jesus. And the New Testament picks up other important themes as well, like when Paul traces our relationship with God through faith alone back to God's relationship with Abraham through faith.

While we're on the New Testament—what's most important there?

I'll give you one guess. . . .

Okay, I know it's Jesus, but are there certain parts of the story that are more important than others?

Yes, there definitely are. In fact, what you emphasize about Jesus is absolutely crucial to your theological lens. I mean, should we prioritize Jesus' teaching, his miracles, his cosmic identity as the Son of God? What you pay attention to shapes your picture of Jesus, which in turn shapes your picture of God.

Great questions. So where are we going to look?

I'm going to suggest that we look to Jesus' cross and resurrection.

Okay, but why?

Three reasons. The first is a historical one. We talked earlier about the development of the New Testament witness to Jesus, with Paul's letters being the earliest Christian writings that we have, then Mark's Gospel, then Luke and Matthew, then finally John.

Right. I remember that Paul was writing in the 50s, Mark around 70, Luke and Matthew in the 80s, and John maybe in the early 90s.

That's right. Well, it gets really interesting when you think that Paul focused almost entirely on Jesus' cross and resurrection. I mean, he knows, or at least tells, almost nothing about the life and teachings of Jesus. He shares no parables, no stories, nothing. About the most we get from Paul is a short theological affirmation about Jesus' humanity: "He was born of woman, under the law."

"Born of woman"? You mean he doesn't even know Mary's name?

If he does, he's doesn't think it's important enough to share.

That's not much to go on.

No, and I think that's because Paul's not really interested in Jesus' life, per se, but rather in the cosmic difference his death and resurrection make.

By the time you get to Mark, though, that has changed. Mark begins his story at Jesus' baptism and then takes us all the way up to the cross and resurrection.

And with Matthew and Luke it's even earlier, because they begin with his birth.

Right. And then you get John, who takes it all the way back to the beginning of time with his clear reference to Genesis, "In the beginning . . ."

Wow. It's like the longer the church had to reflect on the significance of Jesus' cross and the resurrection, the more important they become. First, the church just reflected on the cross and resurrection themselves, but before long it interpreted Jesus' life and ministry through them, then his birth, then the history of the whole world.

Exactly.

So that's the first reason: as the New Testament writings develop, the cross and resurrection increasingly become the important events by which to make sense of all the other traditions about Jesus.

The second reason is what I'd call a literary one—meaning all of the Gospels are clearly structured to point to the cross and resurrection.

In what way?

Take, for instance, all the predictions Jesus makes about his own death. If you read the Gospels as a literary work, it becomes clear these not only foreshadow Jesus' death—and you only foreshadow things that really matter—but they also provide a certain structure to the Gospel stories themselves.

And even in the birth narratives we just talked about, both Luke and Matthew go out of their way to point to the cross.

Really?

Yeah. For instance, in Luke's Gospel, an old man named Simeon, whom Luke describes as a prophet, sees the baby Jesus and says that Jesus "is set for the rise and fall of many," foreshadowing the conflict to come. Then Simeon turns and, speaking directly to Mary, says "and a sword will pierce your own heart also," indicating the pain Mary will feel at Jesus' death.

And Matthew is even more clear, as he has Herod hunting for the baby Jesus right from the beginning. And he's even willing to kill all those other children in the hope of wiping out the baby born to be king. Jesus gets away then, but he won't later on.

I don't think I'd noticed those parts.

We sometimes gloss over them because we want Christmas to be about innocence. That's for good reason, but these darker elements are there too.

Then there's the passion itself, when all the action slows down. I mean, about two-thirds of the Gospels are devoted to Jesus' birth, life, travels, ministry, everything up to when he enters Jerusalem. The last third slows down to give us a nearly hour-by-hour, blow-by-blow account of the events leading up to Jesus' death.

When you start thinking about it, it's hard not to take note of how many things point to the cross.

I agree. Someone once described Mark as "a passion narrative with a long introduction." I think that from a literary standpoint alone you could say that about all four Gospels.

Well, the historical and literary reasons have been so strong I'm not sure you need a third reason, but I'm still curious.

In some ways the third one is the most important. We've talked about history and literature; now it's time to talk theology.

I figured that would come up eventually.

No doubt. And it's really important. Here, I want to go back to Paul, who's the earliest writer in the New Testament. I want to look in particular at a passage in a letter he wrote to the Corinthians.

Which one? There are two letters to the Corinthians, right?

Right. I'm thinking of a passage in the first letter. Paul founded the church in the city of Corinth, but then later left so he could start other churches. At some point after Paul leaves, the Corinthians write to ask him some questions. And one of those is about the resurrection. So Paul devotes most of the 15th chapter to responding to that question. The way he begins this section is really interesting. He starts by saying that he is only reminding them of what he'd taught while he was with them, and then goes on to say:

For I handed on to you as of first importance what I in turn had received:
that Christ died for our sins in accordance with the scriptures, and that
he was buried, and that he was raised on the third day in accordance
with the scriptures, and that he appeared to Cephas, then to the twelve.
(1 Corinthians 15:3-5)

Who's "Cephas"?

That's another name for the disciple Peter.

Gotcha.

For now, I want to focus for a minute on the phrase "For I handed on
to you as of first importance what I in turn had received." Two things
about this are particularly important.

I can guess the first—Paul actually says that this is what's most important.

Yes, and given everything else Paul has taught the Corinthians, that's
a remarkable statement.

The second thing to notice is that he isn't making this up. Paul
says that this is what he himself was taught, presumably when he
was a new Christian. Only twice in all of his letters does Paul make it
clear that he's handing on a tradition he received from others: here
and when he talks about the Lord's Supper in the 11th chapter of the
same letter. So the importance of the cross goes back much earlier
than even Paul. It must already be the center of the theology he has
received and is now promoting throughout the world.

**Alright. I'm convinced—we should start, and maybe even finish, with the
cross and resurrection as the center of our theological lens.**
   One problem, though.

Yes?

**I have almost no idea how that helps me to read the Bible. I mean, okay, so the
cross is really important. I kind of knew that. But how does that help me make
sense of the Bible?**

Not to worry; we're not done yet. Because you're right, simply saying
"cross and resurrection" isn't enough, especially when people interpret the cross in so many different ways.

Like?

Well, some believe the cross stands as the great moral example for all of us to follow, giving our life for another. Others believe the cross should be understood as a sacrifice for sin that makes it possible for God to love and forgive us. Still others think that in Jesus' cross and resurrection God engaged the powers of evil and triumphed over death. In fact, each of these ways of thinking about the cross has a long history and tradition. Taken together, they're known as the three "theories of atonement."

Sounds like another big conversation that maybe we can take up some other time. For now, though, I'm interested in which one is right.

All of them.

What?

And none of them.

Oh, come on!

I'm serious—each one has elements that are theologically valuable and that capture pieces of the biblical witness, and each has elements that I think are more problematic and don't reconcile other parts of Scripture.

So what are we going to do?

Here's my suggestion: let's not try to make the cross fit into a theory. Instead, let's see what the actual event of the cross tells us about God and us.

Sounds good in theory, but I'm not sure I'm following.

Well, I have a suspicion that one of the main problems with these theories is that they all try to fit the cross into a larger plan, as if God had planned everything out long ago and the theologian's job is to figure out the rest of this plan.

You don't think God planned things this way? You think the cross was some kind of accident?

Well, to be honest, I don't know. And you're right, this is probably a longer conversation. But my point for now is that instead of focusing on figuring out how the cross fits into some larger plan, maybe we should just focus on the cross itself and see what it tells us about God, about ourselves, about our life in this world, and so on.

Okay, I'm game.
So what does it tell us?

Lots of things, I suspect, but I think two things, in particular, match up with a whole lot of the rest of the Bible.

What's the first?

The first is that God is holy and we are not, and, when push comes to shove, for that reason God's presence is initially more of a threat than a comfort.

Say that again?

Maybe it will help to look at Scripture.

Good idea.

Okay, let's take three passages quickly.

First, Genesis 3, after Adam and Eve have eaten from the forbidden fruit: when God comes into the Garden of Eden, they are terrified and hide.

Yeah, I remember that story.

What's striking is that before "the fall"—that is, before they sin—they enjoy being in God's company. But now, aware of "good and evil" and recognizing God as completely good, they are afraid.

So one of the things that happens in the fall is that they fear God rather than enjoy being with God.

Right. Because they now know that God is holy and they are not. Second example, when Isaiah has a vision of God in chapter 6, his reaction is despair: "Woe is me! I am lost, for I am a man of unclean lips, and I live among a people of unclean lips; yet my eyes have seen the King, the LORD of hosts!" (verse 5).

But isn't Isaiah one of the great prophets?

Absolutely, but his first encounter with the Lord terrifies him because he knows he can't be in the presence of the immortal and perfect God and live.

Third: Peter's first encounter with Jesus comes after a night of failed fishing; Jesus tells him to throw his net on the other side, and he nets a huge catch of fish. Immediately, recognizing that Jesus is somehow connected to God, his first words are, "Go away from me, Lord, for I am a sinful man!" That's in the fifth chapter of Luke, verse 8.

Okay, I get it, when you meet God, you immediately recognize that God is perfect, holy, and just, and this is a little terrifying. But what does this have to do with the cross?

For that, let's look to John 3:17-20, the verses right after the world's most famous verse.

I would have thought you'd start with John 3:16. That's one of my very favorites.

It's the favorite of a lot of people. In fact, it's probably been translated into more languages than any other part of the Bible.

Okay, let's start there, but we'll read a little further, too:

> For God so loved the world that he gave his only Son, so that everyone who believes in him may not perish but may have eternal life.
>
> Indeed, God did not send the Son into the world to condemn the world, but in order that the world might be saved through him. Those who believe in him are not condemned; but those who do not believe are condemned already, because they have not believed in the name of the only Son of God. And this is the judgment, that the light has come into the world, and people loved darkness rather than light because their deeds were evil. For all who do evil hate the light and do not come to the light, so that their deeds may not be exposed.

I'm still not sure I'm making the connection.

Let me try again: if you want to condense the gospel story down to one sentence, you could sum it up this way: Jesus comes to town preaching, teaching, doing miracles to feed and heal people, and for-giving people their sins—and he gets killed for it.

So what gives? I mean, why does he get killed? Don't most people want food, healing, and forgiveness?

Food and healing, for sure.

But what's wrong with forgiveness?

Okay, I forgive you.

Wait a second, what did I do?!

What does it matter? You just said forgiveness is a good thing, and I forgave you.

Yeah, but I didn't do anything.

So?

So? Well, if I didn't do anything, then who are you to . . .
Oh, I see. Forgiveness is great if you want it, if you know you did some-thing wrong. But if not, it's kind of offensive, like you're accusing me of something.

Exactly. The people in the story who are down and out, who know they are sinful and who aren't generally accepted, think Jesus' for-giveness is just great. But the ones who are in power, the ones who believe they are righteous on their own—thank you very much—find Jesus' words offensive and put him to death. They charged him with blasphemy because he forgave sins, and they believe only God can forgive sins.

So the cross was their way, as John writes, of hating and fleeing the light because their deeds were evil. Or, to put it another way, Jesus made them look bad so they put him to death.

Right. And the cross not only meant that in the past, but it still means that today. That is, the cross shows us what happens when God, the one who is perfectly good and holy, comes to earth—we'd rather run away from this God or, if worse comes to worse, get rid of this God rather than admit that we're broken, sinful, in need of forgiveness.

And this is true even when God comes offering forgiveness?

You saw for yourself. Unless you have some deep sense that you need forgiveness, when someone offers it it feels more like an accusation than help. And for the self-made man or woman of this world, admitting our need for God, our need for forgiveness—really, our need for anything beyond our control—feels like death.

I can see how Jesus' words of forgiveness would be threatening, and still are. So the cross reminds us that we'd rather run away from God than admit that we need God. What's the second thing Jesus' cross and resurrection tell us.

Well, if the first thing the cross and resurrection show us is the truth about our situation, our human condition, then the second truth is about God's response to us.

You'll need to explain this one a bit more too.

No problem. Actually it goes back to John 3:16.

That really is a great verse.

Yeah, it is. Because as brutally honest as John 3:17-20 can seem, you have to keep in mind what comes before it: "For God so loved the world . . . ." According to John, whatever our reaction to God, God's primary disposition, or primary emotion about us, is one of profound love. That is, God comes in love, and even though we reject God, God still loves us. The cross is the testimony to that. God loves us so much, as John says, that God is willing to die on the cross for us.

When I listen to some Christians, it sounds as if Jesus had to die on the cross in order for God to forgive us. Wasn't that behind Mel Gibson's *The Passion of the Christ*?

That film represents one of the three atonement theories we mentioned earlier, where Jesus is seen primarily as a divine sacrifice. Even in this theory, God loves us, but, yes, God can't forgive us until "divine payment" is made and God's sense of justice has been satisfied.

That sounds different than what you were just saying.

It is. Again, there's an element of this theory that is helpful, but essentially I disagree with the idea that Jesus had to die to make it possible for God to love and forgive us. Instead, I'd say that Jesus dies to show us how much God already loves and forgives us. Here it's helpful to turn to Paul, this time to the fifth chapter of his letter to the Romans:

> *For while we were still weak, at the right time Christ died for the ungodly. Indeed, rarely will anyone die for a righteous person—though perhaps for a good person someone might actually dare to die. But God proves his love for us in that while we still were sinners Christ died for us. (verses 6-8)*

That last line is huge: "God proves his love for us in that while we were still sinners Christ died for us." It sure sounds like God isn't waiting for the cross to forgive us. God loves us from the beginning.

Absolutely. And in the resurrection God promises that nothing, not even death, can withstand that love. So when I summed up the Gospels a minute ago, I should probably have added just a little on each end. I'll try again: To show God's great love for all the world, Jesus comes to town preaching, teaching, doing miracles to feed and heal people, and forgiving people their sins, and he gets killed for it, but God, whose love is more powerful than death, raises Jesus from the dead.

That's a pretty good summary. But I still need a little help in understanding how this helps us read the Bible.

Think of it this way. Whenever God comes to town, whenever God gets involved in human affairs, whenever God encounters us, two things happen: first, we learn the truth of our human condition— our need, our vulnerability, our insecurity, our sin—and second, we learn that God loves us in spite of all that and will not stop loving us no matter what.

So Jesus' cross and resurrection tell us two huge truths: the first about our condition and the second about God's response to our condition.

Right.

And these aren't simply fact-truths; they are truths that actually affect you, make a difference for you and in you.

Say more.

Well, no one really wants to hear the truth about being insecure, about being so afraid of God that we'd run away from God or even try to do away with God instead of accepting our problems. But it's only when you do hear that truth that you can hear the second truth. That second truth makes it feel like every-thing is new, like anything and everything is possible.

I agree. When we hear the two truths that the cross and resurrection tell us, we also *experience* the cross and resurrection. Our sense of being able to do it on our own, of not needing God, of pretending we've got everything under control goes away—you could even say it dies. Then we can be raised to new life as we realize that God loves us as we are—not the person we're trying to be or promised to be, but the person we already are. That kind of love gives life.

So God really is love.

The Bible uses exactly those words (1 John 4:8). It's not a sentimental kind of love, but more of a tough love that tells us the truth about ourselves so that we can hear and believe the truth that God loves us.

So to simplify even more: truth #1 is God saying "I know you" and truth #2 is God saying "and I love you."

You've got it.

And God's "I know you" is crucial, because if you don't know that someone really knows you, you can never be sure if the person really loves you.

That's exactly right. And these two truths are not just at the heart of our understanding of the cross and resurrection, but they show us a pattern of what happens every time God gets involved in human affairs.

Even in the three examples from the Bible you used above?

Absolutely. In the Genesis story, even though Adam and Eve fall and must leave the garden, God makes clothes for them and continues to bless and preserve them. In response to Isaiah's awareness of his sinfulness, God cleanses him and then uses him as a prophet to tell the people of God's love. And Peter, as you know, becomes the chief disciple.

Even though he later denies Jesus?

Yes. There's a really poignant scene near the end of John's Gospel where the resurrected Jesus asks Peter if he loves him three times. By the third time Peter is a little upset that Jesus would doubt him, but I think Jesus is giving Peter a chance to affirm his love for Jesus three times to make up for the three times he denied Jesus. And each time Peter answers, Jesus tells him to take care of his sheep, the other disciples.

So Jesus actually gives Peter work to do, kind of commissioning him into a new role and new life.

Exactly. This pattern occurs all over the place: God coming to humankind in love; humans out of fear rebelling or fleeing or rejecting God; God sticking with people—sometimes in judgment, sometimes in mercy, often in both—until people realize just how much God loves them. It's the essential pattern of the Bible that is made most vivid in Jesus' cross and resurrection.

And this serves as our center, our Rosetta Stone, making everything else more clear?

Yes. It's not the only thing that Scripture has to say to us about God, ourselves, and the world, but it's the central testimony. It gives us insight into the heart of God that, in turn, helps us make sense of other passages that seem less clear. It also helps guide us to discern between different interpretations.

But you can't prove this?

No. I mean, I can make a good case for it, but I can't prove it any more than I can prove that *It's a Wonderful Life* is the best movie of all time.

And the fact that I can't prove that we should read the Bible this way is important to remember. This is the confession that is characteristic of the tradition I come from. I think it's actually characteristic of most of the Christian traditions, but each will have its own nuance, and so each tradition will read the Bible a little differently.

And this center, or lens, that you confess helps you make sense of all of Scripture?

It does, although it's important again to not use this or any other lens to make the conversation with Scripture into a monologue. I mean, Scripture has a lot to say about God, and this lens, while very helpful, shouldn't be used to flatten out other things the Bible might want to say.

Can you give me an example?

We've actually worked with one already in our conversation about the meaning of the cross. There are verses that sound like the cross should be an example, that it's a sacrifice, and that it's the place where God engaged and defeats the power of death. All the different theories of atonement start with reading the Bible. Eventually, though, one needs to put all these verses in conversation with each other and with the rest of the Bible and make decisions about what view of the cross is central, which one makes the most sense of the whole, which one seems most in sync with the rest of the story, and which one is most helpful as we try to make sense of our lives here and now.

That doesn't sound like the same thing as saying that just because you view the cross one way you should ignore any verse that suggests looking at the cross another way.

No, it's not. Having a core confession helps you make sense of the whole biblical witness and to discern, at times, between different interpretations. But it shouldn't silence the distinct witness of individual voices. Even with a single author, like Paul, there's a lot going on. A lot of themes and convictions pop up as he tries to work out just what the cross and resurrection mean.

In the end, as helpful as any lens is, we can't afford to assume from the beginning that this is the only thing the Bible has to say to us. The Bible is a rich and diverse book, filled with all kinds of confessions about God, humanity, and the world. We may find that some parts or themes speak more clearly or helpfully to us, but it's important to be open to how God may speak to us differently through the Bible's different parts. That's what we mean when we say the Bible isn't a divine reference book but rather a living Word, a Word that still speaks to us.

That's helpful. And if we start at the center, with the core witness about God's love that tells us the difficult truth about our condition and the wonderful truth about God's loving response, we can really get the conversation going and make sense of a whole lot more of the Bible.

I think so.

Great.

Well, this has answered a lot of questions. But I still have one more.

Only one? I'm a little shocked!

Well, probably more than one, but at least one more really big one.

Sounds interesting. Let's get to it.

Insights and Questions

CHAPTER 7

What Kind of Authority Does the Bible Hold?

So, you mentioned that you have one more major question. I'm curious.

Yes, I do. But I'm not sure exactly how to phrase it. It seems, actually, a little irreverent, maybe even heretical.

Now I'm really curious. Do tell!

But seriously, remember our first rule—no question is dumb. And, I should add, I won't judge you because of your questions. We all have questions, and not only are they important for learning, they're also essential for faith.

Really?

Really. Think about it. Faith is believing something you think is true, but which you don't or probably can't know for sure. I mean, if you could prove it for sure, it'd be knowledge, not faith. After all, in Hebrews 11 the Bible itself says faith "is the assurance of things hoped for, the conviction of things not seen." So in asking questions, we're actually exercising our faith by taking these things seriously, by entertaining possibilities that we can't see. If you have no questions about something, it doesn't really take much faith. That's knowledge, a good thing, for sure, but different from faith.

Look, God can take our questions—even the ones that seem a little weird or irreverent—and so can the Bible. So ask away.

Thanks. I mean that. It seems like a lot of religious people think that doubt is an offense to true faith.

Yeah, I know. But I think it's far from being its opposite. In fact, I'd say that doubt is an essential ingredient to a lively and living faith.

That helps. Okay, so every once in a while when we've been talking about the Bible—how to read it, whether there's a center, and so on—I find myself wondering why we should even bother reading it in the first place. I know that sounds bad, but . . .

No, I actually think it's a perfectly logical question, even if it's one we don't ask much. Maybe, in fact, we ought to ask it more.

Seriously?

Why not? If we're going to spend all this time and energy reading and understanding the Bible, wouldn't it help to know why? Why *is* the Bible important to Christians? And why do we study it? And what are we hoping to get out of our study?

Yes—those are exactly the kinds of things I was wondering about. I know the Bible's important, but I'm not totally sure why. The thing is, if the Bible is the divine reference book like some people think it is, then the question's fairly easy: you read the Bible because it's God's answer book. But if it's not, then the question seems a little more iffy.

That's exactly why I think it's a good question to ask . . . and at the same time a hard question to answer. There are a lot of different answers to this question out there, and certainly in recent history the question of biblical authority—which is what we're now talking about—has divided many Christians.

It does seem as if this is what a lot of churches are fighting about—how to interpret the Bible, especially when it comes to moral issues, and how much, or what kind of, authority it should have.

Yes, these are important and complicated issues, and it seems as if everyone is talking about them these days, so we should too. Perhaps

I can organize our conversation about this around three primary questions: Does the Bible have authority? Where does its authority rest? And why should the Bible have authority in our lives?

I think that sounds reasonable. But I'm not sure I can tell those questions apart. They sound the same. Can you help?

Sure. Let's start with the first and most basic question about whether the Bible even has authority in the first place.

That is pretty basic, although given all of our conversation so far, it seems like kind of a no-brainer.

How come?

Well, of course the Bible has authority. Why else would we be spending all this time trying to figure out how to read and understand it?

I see what you mean. But I still think it's an important question to start with. I mean, we talk about the Bible's authority as if it's a given, but authority is never a given. Something doesn't just *have* authority, it has to receive it.

What do you mean?

Name a few of the persons who wield authority in our world.

Police officers, judges, teachers . . . at least in their classrooms.

Excellent. Now, do any of the persons who hold those jobs have that authority in and of themselves?

Well, no, they have that authority because of the job they hold.

Right, which means the authority they have has . . .

. . . been given to them by the government or school board.

That's true. But even more that, the authority is given to them by the people they have authority over. This is maybe easiest to see when talking about a teacher. Because even though teachers are given authority by the school board, that authority won't mean much if students don't also give that teacher authority. You can hang your diploma in the classroom and talk all you want about the school board, but if the students refuse to be quiet, what does it matter?

And I'd say that's true with police and judges too.

Hold on a second. I can see that a class might undermine the authority of a teacher, but if I commit a crime, I'll go to jail whether or not I choose to give a police officer authority. Seems like that's true whether or not I recognize the authority of the judge who sends me there too.

True enough. Police officers and judges have whole systems of enforcement to back up their authority, but it's the people—the citizenry of a town, state, or nation—that grants that authority through its government.

Which brings us back to the Declaration of Independence.

Hmm?

You know—that governments derive "their just powers from the consent of the governed."

Boy, you really did have a great history teacher.

Thanks. But, seriously, I see what you mean. Authority isn't just out there as some kind of absolute. It arises as people concretely agree to recognize it.

Right. Authority is actually highly relational; that is, it comes in and through relationships in the sense that someone has to "authorize" someone else to get a job done.

And you're saying this is true of the Bible?

Well, let me put it this way. Do you know that saying about "if a tree falls in a forest and no one hears it . . ."?

". . . does it make a sound?" Sure.

Do you know the answer to that question?

Not really.

I don't know either, but I do know the answer to a related one: If a Bible sits on a bookshelf and nobody reads it, does it really have any authority?

I see what you mean. If you're not reading the Bible, it's not likely to have any real authority for you. But does that mean we *make* the Bible authoritative?

Well, on the one hand, Christians confess the Bible derives its authority from its witness to God. At the same time, we give the Bible authority—or at least recognize its authority—only as we read it and take it seriously. So I don't know that we can make it authoritative in general, but we certainly give the Bible authority in our own lives and as we gather with others in our communities. Which means that the Bible's authority, like all authority, is highly relational.

Okay. But what about the part about the Bible receiving its authority from God? That seems important too.

Yes, it is, and here the nut to crack will be how, or in what way, does the Bible receive its authority from God. And that brings us to our second question about where the Bible's authority rests. That is, where do we locate the authority of the Bible, and how do we imagine it exercises that authority?

I'm guessing there are a lot of ways to answer this one too.

There are, because this question gets us into the nitty gritty of our everyday reading of the Bible and what we expect to happen when we read and study it. So to simplify things, I'm going to suggest two primary—and very different—ways to think about the authority of Scripture.

Only two? That reminds me of what Mark Twain once said.

What did he say?

That there are only two kinds of people in the world—people who divide the world into two kinds of people and people who don't!

Well, that's a good caution. There are definitely more ways to think about biblical authority, but the ones I'm going to describe offer two major lines of thought, and most of the other methods tend in one of these two directions.

Sounds good.

Alright. Let's get started by picking a handful of passages. We'll look at how we might think of the authority they hold in each of the two models we're going to explore.

Do you have a favorite passage? We can start with that.

Probably John 3:16, which after our discussion about the center of Scripture seems particularly appropriate.

That's one of my favorites, too, and it is at the heart of things.

Name a couple of others. They don't have to be favorites, just passages you're curious about seeing us work with in terms of biblical authority.

Okay. Let's use the story of creation, too, since so many people seem to get so hot and bothered by that.

Which creation account, though? Just kidding, we'll use both and just call it Genesis 1–2. Name another one.

Okay, how 'bout something from Leviticus.

Where in Leviticus?

Anywhere. I just remember trying to read the whole Bible once when I was still in Sunday school and totally giving up when I got to Leviticus.

I know what you mean. Leviticus contains lots of rules, especially ones that apply to the priests, who were called the Levites because they came from the house of Levi, and so the rules go into a ton of detail about sacrifices and other priestly duties.

I'm already getting sleepy.

Okay, okay, we'll just say "Leviticus" for now. Any others?

Aren't you going to pick any?

Sure. How about 1 Corinthians 11, where Paul talks about the Lord's Supper, and 1 Timothy 3, which talks about qualifications for church leaders.

Probably not what I would have picked, but why not.
That's brings us to five.

That should be enough for our purposes.

Okay. So to make this a little simpler, I'm going to suggest two pictures to represent each of the two models of biblical authority I want to explore. Each one locates the authority of the Bible in a different place. The first picture is of a link chain, where each verse or passage in the Bible is a link in a huge chain.

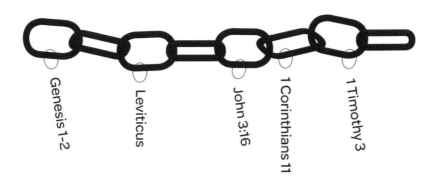

Each verse? That's a pretty big chain.

Which is exactly why we decided to work with only a handful of passages.

The key to understanding this way of thinking about biblical authority is tied to the maxim about chains: "a chain is only as strong . . ."

" . . . as its weakest link."

Right. In this pattern, then, each verse is seen as equally important to all the others, because the authority of the whole Bible is tied to the authority of each one.

So if one passage is seen as less important, as having less authority than others, the authority of the Bible itself is reduced or undermined.

Exactly.

So in our example, Genesis 1–2 is as important as Leviticus, 1 Corinthians, 1 Timothy, and John 3:16. They're essentially all the same.

Or at least they all have the same degree or level of authority and importance. That is, they're all equally valuable for understanding the biblical story of God.

So this is why, then, folks get so hot and bothered about the creation stories being accurate depictions of world history.

Right again. In fact, I remember talking about all this with a classmate in college when . . .

Wait a minute! You talked about biblical authority in college?

'Fraid so.

And it wasn't even for a class, but was "for fun"?

Yeah. I guess that's why I ended up teaching this stuff.

Good career choice!
Okay, so sorry, you were saying you and this friend . . .

Right, a classmate and I were talking about how to take the creation stories—as factual history or symbolic story—when he said, "Sure, maybe it's fine to interpret Genesis that way, but what are you going to do about the resurrection?"

Okay. I see. Your classmate was implying that the creation story in Genesis was as important as the resurrection. No wonder people fight so hard about Genesis.

Absolutely. From this point of view, Genesis feels like the weak link, so folks need to defend it like there's no tomorrow. Because if they surrender this, the whole shooting match is over.

This really reminds me, again, of our earlier discussion about whether the Bible is true.

Definitely. If you operate with a fact-based sense of truth, and you need to prove the validity of the Bible, then every element of your proof is a potential point of vulnerability, and you've got to be able to defend each and every part or risk losing the whole.

So is there an alternative?

There is, but I want to hang on just a minute longer to this one.

How come?

Because I think it's really important to realize what's at stake for folks who hold this understanding of biblical authority. It's easy to criticize people who read the Bible differently than we do, or to shake our heads in dismay at why they defend Genesis as being historically accurate. But I think it's valuable to be able to see where they are coming from. Because if you disagree with someone but don't try to understand why they think this way, all you'll do is butt heads together.

I can see what you mean. It's like we all say the Bible matters, but then we use it in different ways. If we assume we're all using it the same way, we can get pretty frustrated pretty quickly.

Right, and it's important to realize that someone you disagree with might take the Bible just as seriously as you do but understand it differently.

In which case it's probably more important to talk about why we value the Bible and how we understand it first before getting into how certain passages apply to certain issues.

Exactly.

Okay, point taken. Knowing that some, maybe many, people operate with a chain-link view of Scripture will be helpful in trying to understand where they're coming from.
But since I don't think a chain-link understanding is going to work for me, what's the alternative?

I'll describe the alternative with another picture, this time using concentric circles. In this way of thinking, we place the passages of the Bible in a set of concentric circles, with the most important near the center and the others arranged in terms of how important, or central, they are for our understanding of God.

Have you really done that—placed all the passages of the Bible in a big chart? I know we're working with just a few, but do you need to arrange them all?

No. What's most important is having a clear sense of the center. Arranging the rest usually happens in a more ad hoc kind of way when you actually think about what a given passage might mean.

Okay, so in terms of the five passages we're working with, and in light of our earlier discussion, I'd guess that John 3:16 is central.

Not surprisingly, I'd agree. But let's talk a little more about that. You mentioned it's your favorite verse. Why?

Because it's reassuring. It seems to promise that whatever else God is, or whatever else God may feel, love is at the center. I mean, there it is, "For God so loved the world . . ."

I know. And what's even more amazing is that pretty much everywhere else in John's Gospel, when the writer uses the word *world* he means the world that is hostile to God.

Really?

Yeah, sometime read the 17th chapter of John. Essentially, in John's story, the world sees God as its enemy and so essentially hates God. So we might as well translate John 3:16 as, "For God so loved the God-hating world that he gave his only Son."

That's really powerful.

Yeah, it's a really great passage, and I think you're right in that if you're looking for a one-verse summary of the Bible, you won't find much better. I think that's why it's been translated into more languages than any other verse of the Bible.

And probably why you always see it at major sporting events, just where the camera is usually pointing, you know, like behind the umpire.

And all this makes it, I think, a pretty good candidate for being at the center of our diagram of concentric circles.

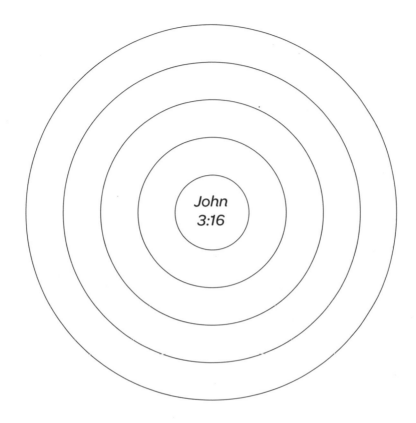

And the other passages?

Well, I'd put 1 Corinthians 11 in the next ring. It's not quite at the center for me, but what Paul has to say about the Lord's Supper is pretty important to our life as a community of faith.

I don't see the rules about who should be a leader in the church as being central, but I imagine they could turn out to be pretty useful at times.

So maybe halfway out on the concentric rings?

That sounds about right.

What about Leviticus?

No question: in the ring farthest from the center!

I'd have to agree. Okay, so what about Genesis 1–2?

Great question. You know, I think it's important to confess that God created the world, so I don't think I'd put those chapters way out on the edge. At the same time, it's not as if I ever wake up in the middle of the night and worry about whether God created the world in seven days or anything, so maybe we should put them about halfway out on the concentric rings too.

So there you have it.

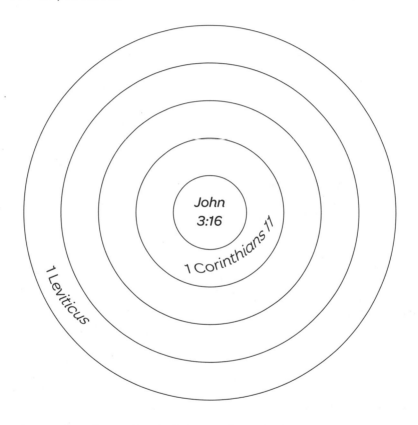

And this is what you do with all the passages?

Again, it's not so formal as this. And, actually, it's not really about the passages themselves, not in this model or the chain-link one. It's more about a larger notion of where we locate the authority of the Bible. In the first model, the Bible's authority is located in its very nature. That is, it has authority because it possesses a certain quality—as a divine reference book it's factually accurate, reliable, and therefore ought to have authority because of what it *is*. In the second model, of concentric circles, the Bible's authority is located in what it does. That is, the Bible has authority because it tells us about the God who loves the world so much. Or maybe better, the Bible has authority because of what it holds, the gospel.

This is what you meant earlier when you talked about a "functional" understanding of biblical authority?

Right. "Functional"—what it *does*, tells us about God—instead of "ontological"—meaning what it *is*, somehow divine and thereby different in its very being from anything else.

So, ultimately, it's God that has the authority, and each of the models propose a way the Bible receives its authority from God. In the link chain model, God gives the Bible authority by making it divine itself, different from everything else. Whereas in the concentric circle model, God more or less retains the authority, and the Bible is authoritative to the degree that it tells us about God.

Right, and I think you actually get a sense of this in the Bible itself. In Matthew 28, Jesus didn't say "all authority in heaven and on earth has been given to the Bible." He said, "all authority in heaven and on earth has been given to me." And so we value and give authority to the Bible because of what it does—it tells us about the God we know most clearly in Jesus.

Hmm.

You don't sound convinced.

No, actually, this makes a lot of sense. In the end, you value anything—a book, a song, a movie—because of what it does, what it holds, what it tells you. The Bible ends up being more important, more of an authority, because the thing it tells us about is God.

So that makes sense, but something about all this kind of bothers me.

Go ahead.

Well, I can understand how important it is to identify what you believe the center of Scripture is, because that helps you make sense of the whole biblical story. But what about the parts that don't seem central or valuable at all, the parts on the outer rings of the circles?

What do you mean?

Take Leviticus. We both agree that Leviticus is, for the most part, pretty boring, kind of hard to understand, and not terribly crucial to the biblical story or to our lives. I don't sacrifice animals, so why should I read Leviticus? And if this is the case, then why not just cut the whole book out?

Or, come to mention it, what about some of the other passages? Like the ones about masters having slaves, or telling women they should be silent. Why not just cut these passages out altogether?

That's a really important question. And it's an option that's been advocated before. Once, in fact, by none other than Thomas Jefferson.

Seriously?

Seriously. Jefferson read the Bible carefully, and because he was very much a child of the Enlightenment and therefore committed to a rational understanding of the universe—that is, everything functioned within certain rational laws—miracles didn't fit into his picture. And so he cut them out—literally—with a pair of scissors.

No kidding?

Everything that defied the laws of the universe as he knew them got cut out, including the resurrection.

I wonder if he thought he was doing the church a favor. Maybe it's because he thought the Bible was important that he wanted to make it rationally acceptable.

You know, in an odd kind of way, Jefferson and the folks who fight about creation aren't all that far apart in the end.

What do you mean?

Well, they both understand the Bible primarily as a logical, rational, modern book, right? They go at it different ways—one cutting out the miraculous parts, the other defending them to the hilt—but they both see the Bible

essentially as something that needs to be proved from the outside if it's going to have any authority.

You're right. I hadn't thought of that, but it's as though they really do start at the same place by thinking that the Bible is a book best approached by reason instead of by faith.

I'm still not sure why we don't do the same thing, though. As Jefferson, that is. Maybe it's not the miracles that offend us; maybe it's the boring parts, or the parts that seem so dated, or even offensive.

Two reasons. First, you never quite know what's going to be important later on. Let's say, for instance, that we decide that all the parts in the Bible that seem to accept slavery as a legitimate practice—which is pretty much most of the passages in the Bible on slavery—need to go.

Sounds like maybe that's not such a bad idea. We could've saved ourselves a lot of trouble about a century-and-a-half ago.

Right. Except that tucked right into the middle of some of the parts on slavery—even in Leviticus—are passages about Jubilee, the periodic release of slaves and debt that God commanded should be a part of Israel's life. And these passages have become incredibly important recently as we think about how to deal with poor nations that owe incredible amounts of money to wealthy nations that just don't need it.

So if you cut out some of the parts, you might lose others.

That's right. The Bible isn't, finally, a collection of little bits of helpful information about God. It's a collection of confessions, a whole library, and so we take together what we feel is helpful and less helpful, clear and less clear, because over the centuries the church affirmed that God was working through this whole crazy family album to communicate God's love and will for us.

Plus, if our reading of Scripture really is more like an ongoing and living conversation than running to the divine reference book, our questions change. So we never know what parts of the Bible will matter to us.

Take Martin Luther, for instance.

He tried to cut parts out too?

Not exactly, but almost. When Luther translated the New Testament into everyday German, he wrote an introduction to each book, and these introductions read almost like report cards.

Who got an "A"?

Paul's letter to the Romans and the Gospel of John. Most of the other books got anywhere from a B to an A-. The book of James, though, essentially got a D-.

You're kidding?

No. He called it a "book of straw" because he thought James's line about "faith without works is dead" was a dangerous challenge to Paul's insistence that we're justified—that is, made right with God— not by our works but by faith.

Later in life, though, Luther got into pretty intense arguments with people who thought that because they were Christians they didn't have to care at all about the law—about helping other people or anything. In those arguments, what James said came in pretty handy. As it turned out, Luther realized that, in some situations, it's critical to emphasize that we're justified by faith apart from the law, but in others, it's just as important to say that faith without works is dead.

Luther's situation and questions had changed, and so different parts of the Bible became more important.

If he'd just cut out James, he wouldn't have been able to go back to it.

Exactly. Cutting something out might work once, but then you've lost it forever.

But there's an even more important reason to stick with the harder parts of the Bible. And it's this: if you understand what the Bible is, you don't have to cut out the challenging parts, even the really difficult passages.

What do you mean?

If we take the Bible as a book of faith—that is, holding confessions of faith that might, in turn, encourage us in faith—then there's no need to prove it, and therefore you don't have to explain the difficult parts away or cut them out. Instead, you recognize stories in the Bible as confessions of faith, confessions that were made by very ordinary people who were gripped by an extraordinary experience of God. Because these confessions were made by real people, they reflect the knowledge, the mindset, and the cultural biases of the people who made them. So while you might not agree with all the details of a particular confession, you can still admire the courage it took to confess and recognize the confession as part of the larger Christian story, perhaps not the center, but still part of it.

So what do you do with the hard parts?

You read them, struggle with them, try to hear them on their own terms, and then make sense of them in light of the larger story. Sometimes you might end up saying, as we did with large parts of Leviticus, that they're not at the center. And sometimes you might actually disagree with a particular confession.

Are you saying some parts of the Bible are wrong?

I'm saying we can acknowledge that all biblical confessions might be faithful, but they don't all hold the same authority because they don't all reflect the central confession of the Bible that has to do with God's incredible love for all the world. Further, because God uses ordinary things like the Bible and ordinary people like the biblical authors, then we shouldn't be surprised if some of those confessions are tied to cultural assumptions we just don't hold any more.

Such as?

We've already touched on one of them when we mentioned the parts of the Bible that make it sound like slavery is acceptable. Other parts include certain views about women and their role in the church and society, and so forth.

In cases like these, we *are* called to make judgments. Not so much judging Scripture but rather judging, or discerning, whether particular passages like these should be valid for us today in light of all the other passages that speak to these issues and about our larger convictions about God that come to us from the whole of Scripture.

So how do you know which passages should hold more authority?

Sometimes you don't. The church has made grave errors in interpretation in the past. And sometimes it takes a really long time. But that, again, is why it's important to read and study the Bible in community. It's not foolproof, but it helps to have others' opinions on this.

Finally, though, you do have to make these kinds of judgments. And the only way you can do it is by reading and interpreting various passages in light of what you believe is the central witness of Scripture about God, humanity, and the world. In this way you can make sense of how the biblical story addresses the challenging issues of our own day.

That sounds like real work.

Sometimes it is real work. But nobody ever said that the life of faith was easy. Rewarding, yes—easy, no.

Now that I think about it, I guess I wouldn't trust it if it were too easy. After all, life is complicated and challenging, and I'm not sure I'd trust you if you had easy answers to making sense of this life.

Although . . .

Yes?

Although it seems like that's what a lot of people are looking for.

Yes, in fact, and to risk Twain's ire again, I sometimes think there are two kinds of Christians in the world. Both think that life is challenging, complicated, fairly turbulent. But where one kind of Christian thinks faith should answer all the questions and make the ground stop shaking, the other thinks faith helps you keep your footing amid the tremors and gives you hope and courage while you try to answer life's questions.

Hmm. I think I'm part of that second group.

Me too.

So, shall we move to our third question?

Sorry, but you're going to have to remind me what that question was.

No problem. We first asked whether the Bible has authority and said that it does to the degree that we read it and give it authority in our lives and faith communities. We then asked where that authority is located and said that we believe the Bible's authority is located in the God it shows us by telling us the story of Israel and the church. This story has its climax in the life, death, and resurrection of Jesus. So now we're ready to ask why the Bible should have authority in our lives—why, that is, we should give the Bible authority.

That does seem like it's at the heart of our questions and conversation.

Then I've got two suggestions as to why the Bible should hold authority in our lives.

Okay, I'm listening.

The first reason I'd suggest takes us back to near the beginning of our conversation, when we talked about the Bible being "our story."

Yeah, I remember. We said that as we read and listen to the Bible it becomes not just some story, but our story. We also said that when we take it as our story we actually become characters in it. We live in light of the characters that came before, and we share in hope of the kind of end the story promises.

Very well said. And that's not only my first, but also my best reason for reading the Bible—it's our story and so it tells us who we are by telling us about the other members of our Christian family.

Like reading the family scrapbook.

Right.

But you can be part of a family and not know much about your family history. And you can be an American and not know much of American history. Does that mean you can be a Christian and not know the Christian story?

That's a good question. What do you think?

Hmm. To tell you the truth, I'm a little conflicted. On the one hand, it seems really important to know the story. I mean, if you don't really know the Christian story at all, it seems hard to talk meaningfully about being a Christian.

At the same time, I have known very little of the Bible for years, and I don't know that I'd want to say that I, and others like me, aren't Christian

because we don't know the Bible. So, yes, I think you can be a Christian and not know much of the Christian story, but I think it's harder.

I think that's an excellent answer. Christian identity comes as a gift from God, and I don't think knowing the Bible or not knowing it can cancel God's promise. At the same time, you're right. You get so much more from that gift and identity when you know what it means. As you know more of the story, that story can become your story, the larger story that helps you make sense of your life.

And the second reason we should read the Bible?

This one might sound a little pragmatic, even a little crass, but I think it's true: we read the Bible because it works.

Huh?

Well, I think that when we read the Bible we're often seeking something.

It seems like a lot of people read the Bible to find values or morals.

Is that what you want to read the Bible for?

To be honest, and again, I feel a little funny saying this, but no. I feel that I have a pretty strong sense of my values. I think I'm looking more for what we've talked about from time to time—you know, more of a sense of how everything fits together, how my life makes sense, how this whole world makes sense, for that matter.

That's why I read it too.

I think a lot of people think religious faith is primarily about morality. Faith does have something to say about morals, but I don't think it's the first or most important thing faith is concerned with.

So what *is* faith most concerned with?

Well, pretty much what you just said—it helps us recognize and deal with the essential mystery that is life and helps us to find meaning in that mystery. Once we have a sense of meaning, then I think it's easier to talk about morals.

From mystery to meaning to morals. I like that.

Thanks. But I think there's still something else that we seek, or at least I seek, when reading the Bible.

What's that?

Faith itself.

Faith?

Yeah, the ability to believe the promises Scripture holds. The ability to believe the story it tells that offers the meaning, purpose, and identity we've been saying we're looking for.

You don't have faith? But . . . but you do this for a living!

Yes, I have faith, but that doesn't mean I don't have questions too. Like you, I wonder about the meaning of life, my purpose here, how to make sense of things.

And, to be honest, when I look around it sometimes feels as if there's a lot more evidence that maybe life doesn't mean anything than evidence that it does. I think it takes faith to believe not only that there's a God who created the world and all the cosmos but also that this God not only knows we exist but actually cares—and cares deeply—about us. Cares about it all—our ups and downs, our successes and failures, our hopes, fears, and dreams.

That's a big part of what the biblical story confesses, and believing it takes faith.

And you don't always have faith? You don't always believe it?

Let's just say that sometimes it's hard; sometimes it's a lot harder than at other times.

Is that the reason you said earlier that doubt isn't the opposite of faith, because you've got doubts too?

Well, I actually do believe that faith and doubt live together. If you can prove everything, it just doesn't make sense to talk about faith. But, yes, it's also my own experience that faith is hard, or at least sometimes fragile.

And so when you say the Bible works, you mean . . . ?

I mean that reading the Bible—and even more, studying the Bible and hearing it preached—encourages me in faith. And I see that happen with other people too.

But not always?

No, not always. You can't determine ahead of time the way it will affect some people or not affect them. To put it in the terms of the Christian story, you can't control the way the Holy Spirit works. All you can do is tell the story and see what happens. But in my own life, and in a lot of other people's lives, when the Bible is read, studied, and preached, people often come to faith or have their faith renewed.

So the two reasons you think people should read the Bible are because it tells us the Christian story and because when people hear it they sometimes come to faith?

Yup. You sound a little disappointed.

Well, no, not disappointed, just . . . Okay, so maybe it's not quite what I thought you'd say. It's just, it's just . . .

Yes? I don't mind; go ahead.

It's just that I thought it would be more concrete, more tangible, more . . .

More something you could prove, or point to, or count on.

Well, yeah, I think so.

Don't worry; you're not alone in that wish. A lot of people want what I'd describe as external proof or validation. If there were just some standard, or some test, that we could administer to the Bible to make sure it was worth believing, things would be a lot easier.

But then it wouldn't take faith.

That's right.

So it sounds as if you're saying you believe Scripture because it has worked in your life. That is, the biblical story rings true for you. It seems compelling, convincing, or persuasive to you.

Yes, that's what I'm saying. In this sense, we might say that the Bible is self-validating. We believe it not because someone outside the Bible has told us to, but because of what the Bible itself has done in our own lives.

And you don't need any external evidence, not even a little bit?

I think once the biblical story has become your story you see all kinds of evidence. That is, you see the truths of the story all around you. You start interpreting life on the terms of the biblical story. And in this way it makes sense of your life and this sense-making-ability is a chief, maybe *the* chief, reason you read and trust the Bible.

Sometimes this happens immediately. A certain story or passage helps you make sense of something going on in your life. And sometimes it takes longer. You might even have to test it out. For example, what the Bible says about forgiveness or about sharing what you have with others might cut across the grain of what you've been taught in your culture. But then you try it out and discover a more rich experience of God and the world.

Ultimately, though, that's all the "evidence" you get—it either helps you make sense of your life or not. And even if you wanted external evidence, where would you look?

This sounds a lot like our conversation about whether the Bible is true.

Yes, it's very much like that.

Essentially, you either want to be able to prove the Bible is true—and you have various ways of trying to do that—or you take it on faith. As I said before, I think the Bible is a book of faith.

Seems like you're saying that's true in two ways.

What do you mean?

Well, first you have to take the Bible on faith, and then as you read and study the Bible it also gives you the faith you need to believe it in the first place.

That's right.

That's not a lot to lean on.

Maybe not, but I think it's enough. I mean, it doesn't prove that the Bible's true, but again, think . . .

. . . of how many things that are important to us that we can't prove. Yes, I remember. And taking the Bible on faith makes more sense to me than making it into something magical or semi-divine.

But how does this all relate to not just whether the Bible is true but whether it has authority in my life?

Well, as we mentioned before, when you believe the Bible you give it authority. That is, as you take the biblical story for your story, you read it more and more, take its claims more seriously, and try to shape your life to fit its convictions, promises, and hopes.

Is this where the issue of morality begins to come in?

Yes, very much. As the story becomes your story, you try to live your life on its terms, by its values. And you try to address your questions— life questions, meaning questions, and morals questions—in light of the story you've heard. That is, as you develop more and more of a Christian identity, you have a stronger sense of what it means to live as a Christian.

That's why many Christians speak of the Bible as their norm, or guide, for faith and life. It shapes both what they believe and how they try to live.

But it's not always easy. There are lots of things that the Bible doesn't speak to directly: everything from what I should do for a living to whether or not nuclear energy is a good thing.

You're absolutely right. This is why putting the meaning-making, identity-creating function of Scripture up front is important. As you gain a sense of the meaning of life, as you develop a sense of your identity as a child of God, you can wrestle with the questions you named, as well as all kinds of other questions.

Once again, it helps to wrestle with these kinds of questions . . .

Let me guess—in community?

Absolutely. When you become a Christian you are joined to a family of believers that stretches from the people in the Bible all the way up to present-day believers. And we can gain a lot from studying what Christians before us have thought and by talking things over with friends today.

Okay, so we believe the Bible because it makes a difference in our lives, and as we take the biblical story as our own story we give it authority to serve as our guide in faith and life. I think I've got it.

You mean "got it" as in "understand it," or "got it" as in "believe it"?

Both, actually. It makes sense to me that God speaks through the confessions of ordinary people to help me make sense of my life and join in the ongoing story of God's mission to love, save, and bless the world. What's extraordinary, when I think about it, isn't so much the collection of confessions that make up the Bible itself. What's most amazing to me is that God wants to include me in all this in the first place and that God would use ordinary people like those in the Bible and those in my church to do all that.

I think you've just captured in a nutshell almost everything we've talked about.

Thanks.

So, what do you think, are you ready now?

Ready for what?

To open the book, to start the conversation, to meet the God of Scripture by reading, questioning, and wrestling with Scripture?

I think so. I feel a lot more confident than before. It helps thinking of it as a conversation for which I don't have to have all the answers or know everything.

None of us does. And another way reading the Bible is like a conversation is that, as with the best conversations, it doesn't end.

What do you mean?

Well, it's like a relationship with a long-time friend. Even though you haven't seen each other for what feels like ages, when you start talking, before long . . .

197

. . . you pick up from where you left off before, as if no time has passed, and soon you're talking about all kinds of things you've talked about before. Yeah, I know what you mean.

The Bible is like that too.

So how 'bout one more passage from Scripture to illustrate this?

Sounds good. Where are we going to go?

This time I want to look at the beginning and end of Mark, the first Gospel to be written.

Okay.

Unlike the other Gospels, Mark gives us very little by way of an introduction. There's no genealogy as in Matthew, no theological reflection as in John, and no formal introduction as in Luke. Instead, Mark essentially gets things rolling with one sentence, and then he's off to the races: "The beginning of the good news of Jesus Christ, the Son of God."

That is fairly abrupt.

Right, and for most of my life I always thought of it as just a not-great opening. After all, Mark was written first, and the other Gospel writers got to build on what he was doing.

But it sounds as if your opinion about Mark has changed. How come?

Well, there's another really abrupt scene in Mark, and it's right at the end.

Actually, there are a couple of endings to Mark, but this is the oldest one.

There are a couple of endings?

Yeah. The oldest manuscripts end at Mark 16:8, but some other manuscripts have two other endings, one shorter and one longer that were added some time later. I want to focus on the oldest and, I think, original ending.

Like the other Gospels, some women are going to the tomb on Sunday morning, and when they get there the stone is rolled away.

They meet a young man in a white robe who says that Jesus has been raised and tells them to go tell the disciples. Then comes the last line of Mark's Gospel: "So they went out and fled from the tomb, for terror and amazement had seized them; and they said nothing to anyone, for they were afraid" (Mark 16:8).

That's it? They didn't tell *anyone*? What's going on?

That's a great question, one that has bugged scholars for years.

More like for centuries. I'm guessing that's why people wrote more endings later.

I think you're probably right. The additional endings are a little more like the other Gospels, with an appearance from Jesus and his commissioning of the disciples. But the oldest ending is more abrupt, more stark.

No kidding. Not only does Jesus not show up, but the women don't even do what they're told.

Well, we know that eventually they told someone, or there wouldn't be a gospel. But, yes, the story itself ends in failure. And I think that's on purpose.

What do you mean?

Two things—first, I think Mark knows that his readers—including us—don't get to see Jesus. All we get is all the women got—a message, a promise. "Do not be alarmed; you are looking for Jesus of Nazareth, who was crucified. He has been raised; he is not here" (Mark 16:6). And so Mark ends his Gospel with characters who are a lot like us, forced to trust only in the promise of Jesus' resurrection.

That's powerful.

Yes, it is, and I always thought that's why Mark ended this way—to leave the women in the same situation we are. But more recently I've thought that maybe Mark was up to something else. Maybe he has the story end in failure in order to solicit our help in bringing the story to a better end, or at least to continue the story.

Say a little more.

Well, the women have heard the good news, but they are paralyzed by their fear. At this point in the story, the readers—you and me—are the only other ones who know the truth about the resurrection and about who Jesus is. In fact, we've known from the beginning who Jesus is, because Mark told us at the outset that Jesus is the Son of God.

Which brings us back to the beginning.

Exactly. Except that now I don't think Mark just botched the introduction. I think that what he really meant is that his whole book, his Gospel, is "the beginning of the good news" and that it's our job to continue the story of the good news. It's our job, that is, to continue the gospel.

You and me?!

Yes, you and me, along with all others who have heard this Word and have been encountered by God through the story of Scripture. We don't have to be perfect—my goodness, none of the people in the Bible ever are.

And given Mark's ending, it sounds as if we don't have to have all the answers, or even be totally confident of our faith.

That's right. I think all we have to do is be willing, be curious, be open to how God might speak to us through God's living Word and use us in God's beloved world.

So what do you think—are you game?

You know, I think I might actually be.

Wonderful, then let's get going.

How should we start?

I've got a suggestion: let's. . .

Let me guess: open the book and join the conversation.

That's as good a way of getting started as I can imagine.

Insights and Questions

Conclusion

There is something odd, even awry, in writing a "conclusion" to a book about entering the biblical story. After all, the Bible invites us to the life of faith, which is a journey. That journey may have a beginning that is unique to each of us, but it has no clear or definite end. Rather, the life of faith is, as we've seen, much more like a good conversation. The best conversations never really come to an end. This is true of the conversations good friends have with each other over the years. Even after being separated by time and space, the strands of the conversation can easily be picked up once again. This is also true of the "big conversations" we have about our deepest beliefs and convictions.

I hope this book has deepened your understanding of and enjoyment of the Bible. I hope you feel you can read it with greater confidence and pleasure. Even more, I hope that it has whetted your appetite for further conversation through reading the Bible on your own, listening to it more appreciatively in worship, and studying it in community.

And if after reading this book you still have questions . . . well, by now you probably know I think that would be a perfectly wonderful thing. Questions are an intimate part of the life of faith and our conversation with the Bible because they are what keep us moving forward. They keep us seeking to learn more and, as we do indeed learn more, we discover that we have more questions to seek after.

Please feel free to be in touch with the publisher of *Making Sense of Scripture*, Augsburg Fortress, with additional questions you have or with suggestions for improving this book. If you want to continue your reading and study, there are numerous Bible studies and other resources available, and some of those are listed in the next few pages. We would welcome your suggestions for additional resources that would help you in your study of the Bible and life of faith.

So while there is perhaps no real "conclusion" to our ongoing journey into Scripture, the time has come to close at least this part of that conversation. Thank you, again, for taking this journey with me into a deeper exploration of the great book of faith we call the Bible. I am grateful for your company.

For Further Reading

Book of Faith Adult Bible Studies. Go to www.augsburgfortress.org

Charpentier, Etienne. *How to Read the New Testament.* Crossroad, 1982.

Charpentier, Etienne. *How to Read the Old Testament.* Crossroad, 1982.

Drane, John. *Introducing the Bible.* Minneapolis: Augsburg Fortress, 2005.

Fretheim, Terence. *About the Bible.* Rev. ed. Minneapolis: Augsburg Fortress, 2009.

Hiers, Richard. *The Trinity Guide to the Bible.* Trinity Press International, 2001.

Jacobson, Diane, and Robert A. Kysar. *A Beginner's Guide to the Books of the Bible.* Minneapolis: Augsburg Books, 1991.

Jacobson, Rolf, Karl Jacobson, and Hans Wiersma. *Crazy Book: A Not-So-Stuffy Dictionary of Biblical Terms.* Minneapolis: Augsburg Books, 2009.

Koester, Craig. *A Beginner's Guide to Reading the Bible.* Minneapolis: Augsburg Books, 1991.

Lutheran Study Bible. Minneapolis: Augsburg Fortress, 2009.

Powell, Mark Allen. *Fortress Introduction to the Gospels.* Minneapolis: Fortress Press, 1998.

Rediscovering the Book of Faith. Minneapolis: Augsburg Fortress, 2008.

Olson, Stan, Mark Allen Powell, and Diane Jacobson. *Opening the Book of Faith.* Minneapolis: Augsburg Fortress, 2008.

Powell, Mark Allen. *How Lutherans Interpret the Bible.* DVD. Select Multimedia Resource.

Theissen, Gerd, and John J. Bowden. *Fortress Introduction to the New Testament.* Minneapolis: Fortress Press, 2003.